THRIVING IN A PUBLIC SCHOOL

ALLEN LEVIE

TABLE OF CONTENTS

ACKNOWLEDGMENTS

Thank you to the students of Horlick High School, whose enthusiasm, work, and hope gave life to this book.

A special thanks goes to Edward McDonald, who not only provided moral support but whose critique kept me focused on the essentials. His unwavering support for this body of work motivated me to complete it.

The stories and lessons told within the book would not have been possible without the unflinching support of Christine Neuman Ortiz and Voces de la Frontera.

My son, Dan Levie, and his company, Austin Design Lab, were invaluable in guiding the journey from manuscript to a published book.

The content and experience shared are owed to the 70 people I interviewed, who patiently recounted their part in the story and who shared the wisdom they gained:

Aaron Eick
Alan Hutton
Alexis Gates
Alvin Levie
Ambria Golden
Ambrosia Golden
Anthony Brulport
Ari Antreassian
Bernice Beltran
Beverly Hicks
Bianca Quintera
Breana Scott
Breana Stephens
Brenda Garcia
Brianna Horton
Brittnay Calloway
Brittney Brown
Cecilia Anguiano
Cecilia Leal
Dillion Straube
Don Neilson
Elliot Magers
Elliot Turner
Edward McDonald
Fernanda Jimenez
Galen Horton
Gabriel Coronado
Giselle Becerra
Jacqueline Loiacono
Janet Serrano
Jarasha Williams
Jeff Longsine
Jennifer Levie

Jessika White
John Lehman
Jose Garcia
Jose Rivera
Julie Mckenna
Kamala Richards
Kate Werning
Kennia Coronado
Kevin Brown
Kristina Folk
Kristin Althoff
Larry Miller
LaQuita Barker
Lizeth Brito
Lousia Morales,
Lucero Rocha
Luis Tapia
Maranda Mac
Maria Morales
Maria Vital
Melanie Benish
Melissa Zeien
Nola Starling-Ratliff
Robert Peterson
Rubin Ramos
Sandra Gomez
Sergio Anguiano
Stephon Chapmon
Stephan Kalmar II
Talitha Gudal
Tara Harris
Trisha Young,
Viridiana Rocha
Viviana Pastrana
Yasmin Osorio
Yesenia Sanchez
Xavier Marquez

The completion of the book was made possible by the quality contributions, editing and professional expertise provided by the following colleagues, all brothers and sisters in the struggle:

- Melissa Zeien (Formatting and Final Editing)
- Allen Ruff, Keith Kohlman (Initial Editing)
- Aaron Eick (Contributing Content and Editing for Accuracy)
- Ari Antreassian (Research)
- Fernanda Jimenez (Administrative Support)
- Jennifer Levie (General Support)
- Jacqueline Loiacono, Kevin Brown (Teaching and Learning Consultants)

This book is dedicated to my mother and father Edith and Alvin Levie. Their commitment and devotion to fighting for a better world served as an inspiration and example to me and my siblings. As a result, we have all tried to make the world more humane and just.

BACKGROUND

Racine

Racine, in many ways, is similar to other former midwestern manufacturing centers that today are categorized as post-industrial (rust belt) cities.

It was once a prosperous small city of 80,000 people. There were large migrations of immigrant and African American workers from the South to fill the demands for labor from the major manufacturers. Workers formed unions and were some of the highest-paid workers in the county. The schools, parks and public services reflected the boom that Racine was experiencing.

Eventually, globalization undermined the health and vitality of the Racine economy, just as it did many manufacturing centers across the United States.

Three events accelerated the decline of manufacturing in Racine alongside other rust belt communities.

They were:

1. **The North Atlantic Trade Organization (NAFTA)**
    a. Established in 1994, this agreement was an attempt to set up a free trade zone with Canada, the United States and Mexico in order to rival the European Common Market. It moved millions of union jobs to Mexico in exchange for cheaper goods.
2. **The World Trade Organization (WTO)**
    a. Established in 1995, the WTO created a worldwide membership-based trade organization that facilitated trading

rules whereby countries had to abide in order to take part in the organization. This body accelerated multinational corporations' ability to search the globe for the cheapest labor sources and undercut the ability of US based companies to manufacture their products stateside. Governments who did not comply with the terms of the trade agreements faced huge fines. To avoid the fines, the U.S. complied. Complying led to the flooding of cheap products into U.S markets and the loss of millions and millions of good-paying manufacturing jobs.

3. **China's Most Favored Nation Trading Status (MFNS)**

    a. On December 27, 2001, the United States government granted China MFNS status. It paved the way for China to be part of the WTO. From 2001 onward, the United States lost millions of additional manufacturing jobs.

The impact of these events on Racine cannot be overstated. Major employers either closed up shop or moved elsewhere; they could not compete. Racine became a center of high unemployment. For most of my tenure at Horlick, it had the second-highest unemployment rate in the state.

With the decline in manufacturing jobs came a shift in the demographics and a decline in city living. The poverty rate increased, tax revenue decreased, and the schools had less money to provide for students to receive a quality public education. Working-class white, black and brown families shouldered the brunt of the economic downturn.

Racine Unified School District

During its period of relative prosperity, in 1962, the Racine Unified School District (R.U.S.D.) was formed by combining all public rural and urban schools in Racine County east of the newly-constructed Interstate 94. New modern schools were built in growing suburban areas to replace the old rural school buildings and ease existing schools' overcrowding; decades of redlining had created nearly all-White neighborhoods in the suburban areas. These areas received the new schools, while the children of the Black families moving into older urban neighborhoods attended the 19th-century schools. At the time, RUSD was one of the top public-school districts in the nation for student achievement and a national leader in program and curriculum development. Students in the suburban elementary schools had access to art, music, gym, and library programs staffed by full-time certified teachers. Junior high and high schools provided instruction in art, music, radio & television, theater, all manner of vocational training, clubs, and a wide variety of interscholastic sports. However, the inner-city elementary schools did not enjoy the same treatment.

Gains were won as a result of struggle on the part of parents, the community, and the union.

In the late 1960s and early 1970s, Black residents protested the pervasive inequality in the distribution of city services, including housing discrimination, and learning conditions for minority students. Black neighborhoods had rundown community centers, while several new ones were built in White neighborhoods. After the Lakeview Community Center was firebombed, city leaders feared the rising tensions would lead to riots. As a result, they soon built two new community centers in the central city neighborhoods.

The African American and Latino communities' demand that high school courses in Black History, Latino History, and Black Literature be established came to fruition. These classes were open to all students, and the teachers and students created a broader culture of learning and respect within the schools.

In 1975, after many years of resistance and under the threat of looming legal action, the Racine Unified School Board desegregated the junior high and elementary schools by redrawing the attendance boundaries and busing a limited number of inner-city students to the suburban schools.

In the 1970s, many Latino families settled permanently in Racine. They pressured the Racine Unified School Board to create a K-12 dual language program for all students, but the board voted down the proposal. After the meeting, an 11th grade student confronted school board member Bernice Thompson. After a verbal exchange, Mrs. Thompson slapped the girl across the face and yelled, *"Shut up, you dirty Mexican!"* The local newspaper widely covered this incident, and the school board imposed a penalty of censure on Mrs. Thompson. Still, she was re-elected several times and remained on the school board, which set educational policy for the district.

The teachers had their own struggles for improving conditions in the school. Their well-being was disregarded. When unmarried women approached the school board to ask for health care benefits, they were told by the board president to get married and join their husbands' plans. In the 1950s, female teachers were forced to resign if they married or became pregnant. Teachers banded together to build power in the teachers' union, the Racine Education Association (R.E.A). Working conditions and terms of employment led to job actions and teacher strikes, culminating in the strike of 1978, which became the longest teacher strike in U.S. history at the time. As a result, teachers made significant gains in their wages and working conditions. Their collective action left an indelible mark on their consciousness. With their newly acquired power, they exerted their influence on teaching and learning in the district.

William Horlick High School

Horlick is one of the three comprehensive public high schools in Racine, servicing the North side of the city of Racine and Racine County. It opened its doors on September 17, 1928 on land donated by William Horlick, the original patent holder of malted milk. In 1929, its enrollment was just over 400 students. In 2000, when I began teaching at Horlick, its student population had grown to around 2,200. It was extremely diverse, both economically and racially. Its population included students from some of the poorest families as well as from some of the richest. Latinos and African Americans comprised around 49% of the total student population, in near equal numbers, and white students around 49%. The other 2% were Asian, Native American and other groups.

Influential Community Organizations

The following community organizations were central to the community building components referred to in this book:

VOCES DE LA FRONTERA

Voces de la Frontera is a Wisconsin membership-based community organization led by low-wage workers, immigrants, and youth whose mission is to protect and expand worker, civil, and student rights through leadership development, community organizing, and empowerment. Voces strives to create a world where all people live free of poverty and discrimination, have access to safe, dignified work, quality education, and health care; where immigrants can cross borders with dignity; and human rights and workers' rights are respected; where government is truly "of the people," and where all families thrive.

The school-based student chapter of Voces at Horlick does so with the full support of the organization, and the students are incorporated into the decision-making bodies of Voces.

NATIONAL ASSOCIATION FOR THE ADVANCEMENT OF COLORED PEOPLE (NAACP)

The N.A.A.C.P. was established in 1909 and is America's oldest and largest civil rights organization. It was formed in New York City by white and Black activists, partially in response to the ongoing violence against Black Americans around the country. The mission of the N.A.A.C.P. is to achieve equity, political rights, and social inclusion by advancing policies and practices that expand human and civil rights, eliminate discrimination and accelerate the well-being, education, and economic security of Black people and all persons of color. The Racine chapter was organized in 1967 and has embraced and assisted in student organizing at Horlick High School.

PREFACE

This book tells the story of how students, educational workers, and their allies struggled to change an educational system that was not only designed to benefit the few at the expense of the many, but practiced institutional racism. It explores how divisions that were created by the educational system were overcome by working on social justice issues in the school and communities in which the students resided.

In 1903, W.E.B. Dubois, in his book, "The Souls of Black Folks", wrote, *"...the problem of the Twentieth Century is the problem of the color line."*

The perpetuation of racial inequality is a 21st-century reality.

Our schools, by design, are the pipeline for perpetual social and economic inequality in the 21st century. Racism drives that inequality. It is an ideology that has at its core the premise that one group is superior to the other, even children. It provided the necessary rationale for the inhumane treatment of enslaved Africans. With the advent of the Industrial Revolution, racism continued to be used to divide workers to maximize profits.

These false ideologies and acts laid the foundation for institutionalizing racism in all aspects of life, such as where people could live, what jobs they could hold, and what types of education were accessible.

Delores Huerta once said, *"Every moment is an organizing opportunity that can bring people together, every person is a potential activist, every minute is a chance to change the world that changes begin with bringing diverse people together for the common good."*

Through this organizing and activism, gains in law around civil rights, civil liberalities, integrated education, fair housing, workers' rights and wealth creation were realized. Equally as important, organizing and activism produce civic engagement, which is the backbone and bloodline of a democracy.

William Horlick High School, where I taught students for 19 years, is like most public schools, a racist institution, because it and the school district are guilty of producing racism and facilitating systemic racism by maintaining the status quo. Horlick existed and operated within a larger societal context. The school system caters to the children of parents with wealth and power. My work in the school came to involve helping students from a lower socio-economic class overcome barriers, thereby building an awareness that they could collectively act on the injustices they faced within the schools and the larger society and ultimately gain power.

This book's basic premise is that learning is a political act, and that this learning does not take place in a vacuum. Rather, in acting to improve their teaching and learning conditions, students develop a political understanding of the obstacles to their success and affect change. In working with my students in this way at Horlick, I saw how their action changed them and how it allowed for political growth. This political growth had far-reaching implications on a personal and collective level. It not only allowed for real academic success to take place, but had far-reaching consequences in students' life choices and career paths.

The process of writing this book involved interviewing over 70 people, mostly former students.

You will hear from them in their own voices.

INTRODUCTION

I decided to become an educator at the age of 33. My mother, who taught in the working-class public school district of East Hartford, Connecticut for over 25 years, had a big influence on my decision to become a teacher. Before teaching, she was a stay-at-home mom who raised four children. She finished her college education a year after I graduated from high school and landed a job at the same high school I had graduated from. At age 40, she had arrived. She came into the job with lots of worldly experience. Her students loved her. Like her, I also arrived at teaching late. I began my college education at age 33. I thought that perhaps my experiences could help provide my students with a rich learning environment, as had my mother's. Upon completion of my teacher training, she gave me advice that proved to be invaluable. She said, *"Allen If you put your students first and the subject matter second, you will have a rewarding and meaningful teaching experience."*

Despite my mother's beautiful advice, during my first semester of teaching, I completely forgot her wisdom, and instead, using all of the tools I had learned in teacher training, focused solely on the delivery of instruction. It was a rough and rocky road. On a daily basis I struggled to deliver what I thought was meaningful and thoughtful instruction. It took another year of slowly learning the material and honing my craft to relax enough to begin to connect with the students. Only then did my mother's advice begin to resonate. I started connecting with students on a meaningful level. I began to catch glimpses into their thinking and their aspirations. We became comfortable with each other, and I quickly became a respected teacher with a good reputation. During my first two years of teaching, I spent time sizing up my school, analyzing how it functioned and for whose benefit. It became crystal clear to me that building relationships with the students and assisting them with their learning was not enough.

My urban school was a microcosm of the world I had spent most of my life trying to change in a positive way. The school's mission was to socialize students and to mainstream them into careers as obedient workers. What also became clear to me was that it perpetuated the status quo. The same inequities and class divisions that existed in society existed in the school. The hierarchy of the school and the school system were, and still are, based on a corporate model.

Students and staff all exist within this system. I began noticing that for students, educational opportunities were unequal. There existed a hierarchy of learning and enrichment activities. School workers, too, operate within that same system. Teachers, social workers, paraprofessionals, janitors, kitchen workers - they were all part of that hierarchy.

My growing awareness that the educational system was designed to benefit the few at the expense of the many and that racism, gender, and class division were woven into the school began to dictate my role within that institution.

It became clear that in order to change the system, students and educational workers needed to build their power. There is an old saying among teachers - *"a student's learning environment is the teacher's working environment."* Students and teachers share the same interests. They share the same space. Staff and students can only create better, more equitable schools and a more equitable society by struggling together for positive change.

This book will explore the vast amount of growth and learning that took place among the students and staff at Horlick. Some were more obvious than others, such as critical thinking, communication, writing, and organizational skills. Others less tangible, such as hope, compassion, and confidence, all of which changed the culture of the school, the relationships between students and school staff, and student and teacher success.

I will share some of my experiences in student and teacher organizing and the intersections of the two groups. By highlighting some of the major events that the students were involved in, I will show how these activities provided agency for the students, how the students began to organize for power, and how staff stood alongside them and became involved with that organizing.

I will show how the struggle to change conditions impacted both students and teachers. While we lost more battles than we won, through our work and through our collective struggle, we were ultimately victorious. Defining victory is the key to understanding the profound impact of organizing in schools by students and teachers.

In this book, we will explore the victories.

While teachers clearly have more power than their students within the traditional school hierarchy, the key to building real power for both teachers and students lies in their degree of collective consciousness, in their willingness to act, and in their ability to identify and develop allies through their struggle.

Devalued and demoralized teachers often blame students and their families for low achievement. Conversely, alienated and frustrated students often blame teachers for their lack of success or interest in school.

Rarely do they recognize the fault in the system in which they both work and learn.

When they do, real change is possible.

PART 1

2001-2011

CHAPTER 1

LEARNING THE ROPES

In my work as a teacher, I came to understand that public schools reflected the class nature of the larger society. We were educating future leaders, training future workers, and marginalizing the poor.

It was an affront to my sense of social justice.

In December of 2000, I was interviewed for a social-studies teaching job at Horlick High School in Racine, Wisconsin. I began working at Horlick in January 2001. Prior to my work as a Social Studies teacher at Horlick, I had a multitude of jobs. I worked as a structural steel worker, a machinist, a political and community organizer, and in a prison service organization as a job's trainer and coach. The breadth of my work experience and union activity gave me a varied assortment of skills and knowledge that were utilized at Horlick. While the workplaces were vastly different, they all operated within the framework of one overall socioeconomic system: Capitalism.

My work experiences armed me with the perspective that people can affect change in the environments in which they work.

In looking back with great fondness at my efforts to impact my working environment, many stand out. To illustrate my point, however, I'll retell one. Fresh out of high school, I went to work for a general construction contractor as a general laborer. My strongest suit on the job was structural steel work. I was required to bolt together the steel frames of the buildings. We would erect the steel building columns and beams and then connect them with steel purlins, horizontal structural members in the roof. This was hard and dangerous work. A structural steel worker had to contend with working dozens of feet off the ground on unstable structures. Not everyone is cut out for that type of work. In my case, however, having been a two-time state champion wrestler, I was well-equipped for the job. I was strong, agile, and performed well in the face of adversity. I loved a challenge. My employer valued my abilities. Even though it was over fifty years ago, I'll never forget the incident. It was on a Sunday morning. The company had rented a special crane with enough boom to lift the beams in place on a building taller than most of the buildings we constructed. Our regular crane could not handle the job.

The crew and I showed up to start working. I asked one of the crew members how much money we were going to be paid for working on a Sunday. He told me the company only paid regular pay because it was a new week. I told my fellow workers that this was the seventh day in a row that we were asked to work and we should receive double time. I asked if they were willing to walk off the job if we didn't receive the overtime. Some said they would. So, around an hour after we started, I told the foreman he either needed to pay us double time or we were all leaving at noon. He walked away, muttering to himself. Twenty minutes later, the big boss showed up. I was twenty-five feet up, connecting two beams with a purling, when I heard the foreman tell the owner that Levie and some of the crew were leaving at noon if we didn't pay them double time.

The owner responded, "Can we complete the job without them?"

The foreman replied, "No."

The owner said, "Pay the sons of bitches."

We never heard another word about it. At nineteen-years-old, I learned that workers had power. That power came from their collective willingness to withhold their labor strategically.

In January of 2000, I started my high school teaching career at Horlick, an inner-city school with over 2,000 students. As mentioned in the preface, it was extremely economically and racially diverse. There were an equal number of Black and Latino students, each comprising approximately twenty-five percent of the population, most working class and poor. The White student population hovered around 50%, most of whom were working-class and poor as well.

When I began teaching in 2001, students were essentially divided into four learning tracks. The first of which was the basic classes, consisting of low-level learners, students who were generally from poor families, students who had cognitive or emotional disabilities, or students who were generally not engaged in their learning.

Second, there were regular classes, which were composed of students who essentially, for the most part, were not interested in college. These classes were more academically rigorous than the basic classes, and more often than not, the students in these classes would go directly to work or enroll in a local technical college after graduation.

The third track was known as college prep. The classes in this track consisted of mostly white students from working-class and middle-class backgrounds. The students enrolled in these classes faced more rigorous work than in the previous two tracks and were college-bound.

And lastly, there were the advanced placement classes. This track consisted mainly of white students of the middle and upper middle classes. These classes were not necessarily more rigorous than the college-prep classes, but students could earn college credit for passing an exam at the end of the class. These courses were offered as an attempt to dampen down the white flight from the public high schools by catering to the sons and daughters of those higher up on the social and economic scale.

My four years of teacher training did not prepare me for the first day on the job. I was starting mid-year, teaching five classes at three different course preparations. During my first year, I taught regular World History, Sociology, and African American History as an elective. I started mid-year because the previous teacher had fallen ill and could not continue. The class I inherited was predominantly worksheet-driven and grades were calculated based on the completion of the worksheets; it was in a sad state of affairs. It was gloomy. The walls were dirty and had holes in them. There were decades of papers and projects piled up all over the room and in the closet.

Although I prepared what I considered to be brilliant lessons, the students by and large were resistant and disengaged. Maintaining discipline was next to impossible. Despite my years of work experience as well as the excellent professional training I received at UW-Milwaukee, I had a hard time engaging the students and maintaining classroom order.

To say my first semester of teaching was more than a challenge is an understatement.

At a low point after a particularly challenging 10th-grade World History class, I remember thinking, *I'll be damned if I let these little bastards drive me out of here.* I had to call on my fifteen years of work experience and high self-esteem in order to survive.

I spent the first three years at Horlick improving my skills, practicing my craft, getting to know the students and becoming involved in the teacher's union in the building. I attended all of the monthly building meetings where we discussed both building and district-wide work issues. I became a union representative in my third year, and during my fourth year, I became the building president when I agreed to finish out the year for our previous president, who was experiencing health issues that prevented her from finishing out her term.

Like most new teachers, I learned how to teach and attempted to motivate my "regular" students to learn. I found that building strong personal relationships with the students was a key ingredient to getting these working-class kids engaged. When I wasn't in the classroom teaching, I was in the hallway greeting kids or in the cafeteria sitting and eating lunch with students. I attended many of the after-school activities such as football and basketball games, wrestling matches, and theater productions. I tried to let the kids know that I cared about and was interested in them.

Over time, I further understood that public schools reflected the class nature of the larger society. My urban school was a microcosm of the world I had spent most of my life trying to change in a positive way. The school's mission was to socialize students and to mainstream them into careers as obedient workers. What also became clear to me was that it perpetuated the status quo. The same inequities and class divisions that existed in society existed in the school. The hierarchy of the school and the school system were, and still are, based on a corporate model.

Students and staff all exist within this system. I began noticing that for students, educational opportunities were unequal. There existed a hierarchy of learning and enrichment activities. School workers, too, operated within that same system. Teachers, social workers, paraprofessionals, janitors, kitchen workers - they were all part of that hierarchy.

Similar to the students, the teachers were also divided. It seemed like those teachers who bought into the dominant culture and ways of thinking not only reflected those principles in their classes, but were paired up with students who shared those same values as well.

I noticed the massive division that existed not only in the student body but among the staff as well. Most teachers aspired to teach the Advanced Placement and College Prep classes, knowing that they had to appease their department chairs (who were appointed by the Directing Principal) in order to do so.

Our Social Studies department chair fit nicely into this mold. Two young fellow teachers who started teaching at Horlick six months after I did were given the AP Psychology and AP History classes to teach. Both held Bachelor's Degrees, were fairly new teachers, appeared traditional in their outlook, and had no experience teaching in an urban school district. Kevin Brown, an African-American teacher with a Master's Degree in Psychology, and several years of teaching experience, was not even considered for these classes. Years later, I asked Kevin why he didn't apply to teach the AP Psychology classes.

He replied, "When I inquired about the job, I was told that it was already filled."

I suspect he was not considered because he taught from an Afro-centric perspective.

As in the case of Kevin, I was not cut from the kind of cloth that would lead to teaching what was considered by the administrative team as the plum classes. I was relegated to doing hard time; that is, teaching the regular classes.

I came to thrive teaching the students in those classes.

My growing awareness that the educational system was designed to benefit the few, at the expense of the many, and that racism, gender, and class division were woven into the school began to dictate my role within that institution.

It became clear that in order to change the system, students and educational workers needed to build their power. There is an old saying among teachers - *A student's learning environment is the teacher's working environment*. Students and teachers share the same interests. They share the same space. Staff and students can only create better, more equitable schools and a more equitable society by struggling together for positive change.

This book will explore the vast amount of growth and learning that took place among the students and staff at Horlick. Some were more obvious than others, such as critical thinking, communication, writing, and organizational skills. Others less tangible, such as hope, compassion, and confidence, all of which changed the culture of the school, the relationships between students and school staff, and student and teacher success.

I will share some of my experiences in student and teacher organizing and the intersections of the two groups. By highlighting some of the major events in which the students were involved I will show how these activities provided agency for the students, how they began to organize for power, and how staff stood alongside them and became involved with that organizing. I will show how the struggle to change conditions impacted both students and teachers. While we lost more battles than we won, through our work and through our collective struggle, we were ultimately victorious. Defining victory is the key to understanding the profound impact of organizing in schools by students and teachers.

In this book, we will explore the victories. While teachers clearly have more power than their students within the traditional school hierarchy, the key to building real power for both teachers and students lies in their degree of collective consciousness, in their willingness to act, and in their ability to identify and develop allies through their struggle.

Devalued and demoralized teachers often blame students and their families for low achievement. Conversely, alienated and frustrated students often blame teachers for their lack of success or interest in school. Rarely do they recognize the fault in the system in which they both work and learn. When they do, real change is possible.

CHAPTER 2

LAYING THE FOUNDATION

"Hell no, I'm taking tomorrow off and joining the immigrant freedom marchers at City Hall"

YESENIA SANCHEZ, SOPHOMORE, HORLICK HIGH

During my third year, an incident put me on the path to student organizing. The teacher who taught Latino American History left at the end of my second year. Although she was a seasoned teacher, she struggled to connect with the students, often lamenting about how she worked hard to make the lessons relevant, but the students weren't responding. The vast majority could not stand up to the rigor of her lessons and chose not to complete them, ultimately failing the class. When she spoke about her disappointment in the students, I thought maybe it wasn't the students at all but the relationship between the teacher and the students that stood in the way. I believed my approach would bear fruit.

I asked the department chair to assign the class to me. I thought for sure he would; after all, no one else was even remotely interested.

He replied, "We are not going to offer that class next year. We don't get a big enough bang for our buck." He explained that enrollment at the beginning of the semester was around thirty students, but only two or three students ever passed the class in a semester.

I told him I would put together a plan to make the class successful and asked him if he would offer it the following year if I did. He agreed. I put the plan together and showed it to him, and he approved the course. I immediately began implementing my plan, the core of which was to build relationships with some of the most popular and boisterous Latino students, most of whom were members of the wrestling team, who comprised about half of the squad. I had been a two-time state champion wrestler in high school, and despite being forty-five years old, (and over the hill by wrestling standards), I could still hang with these athletes.

After many playful physical challenges, bumps and bruises, I succeeded in building strong relationships with these students.

The second part of my plan was to team-teach the class with a very popular Latino bilingual teacher. The third part was to work with the district to revise the curriculum.

Ultimately, when it came time to offer classes for that year, Latino-American History was not listed. I informed my department chair, stating that it must be a mistake because he had previously approved my plan.

The department chair parroted his original response to me, saying, “We don’t get a big enough bang for our buck.”

I reminded him about my preparation plan for the class and his approval.

He responded, “Why did [you] think that [you] could do any better than Sue?”

Sue was the teacher who had previously taught the class. He had pitted us against each other, but rather than accept his answer, I made the decision to bypass him. I went over his head to the directing principal to advocate for the class.

To my surprise, she said to me, “It’s part of the district curriculum, so if enough students sign up for the class, it will be offered.”

I encouraged the Latino wrestlers to sign up for the class and to spread the word. They did as I asked; the enrollment numbers were over twenty-five, and the class was on.

The Latino History class started like any other. There was the “getting to know you” phase, the outlining of expectations, and time spent providing an overview of the course curriculum. It was a lively class but a respectfully engaging one. One of my star pupils, Xavier Marquez, was a good wrestler and a very popular student. I had a great relationship with him. During wrestling practices, I wrestled with him and helped coach him. Xavier had grown up with and was friends with most of the students in the class. He made sure the other students respected me and gave me a chance. He provided me with "street cred." With time and with work, the students had no problem allowing a White middle-aged man to teach them about their history.

My goal in teaching the class was to help the students cope with their oppression - to rise above it. I focused on issues of race, class, and oppression. Immigration played a central role in the curriculum. The vast majority of students were either immigrants or first-generation children born in the U.S.

As part of the immigration unit, I showed a PBS documentary about the impact of immigrants, mainly from Mexico, on a small southern town that had a Tyson poultry slaughterhouse. It showed how Tyson actually put in orders for "coyotes" to usher Mexicans without papers across the border and back to their small towns. As the immigrant population grew in the south where the documentary took place, there were those among the long-term residents who became upset. They detested the music, the vibrance of the culture, and the presence of the immigrants. In response, the Ku Klux Klan began to organize and hold rallies there.

In watching and processing the documentary, the unfairness of it all was too much for my students. They heavily identified with the immigrants.

Racine, Wisconsin has in its own history an active Ku Klux Klan chapter.

Photo: Wisconsin Historical Society

From the back of the room, a student named Yesenia, waving a flier, yelled out, “Hell no! I’m taking tomorrow off and joining the immigrant freedom march at city hall!”

Many of the students nodded their heads in support.

That day, I got on the phone with my new principal. I told her about the immigrant freedom march, and that I wanted to take the students on a field trip to participate. She agreed, and the next day a group of students, alongside myself, my wife, and our baby, joined the march.

It was a small demonstration in front of the Racine County courthouse. It was at this march that I met Christine Neuman Ortiz, Executive Director of Voces de La Frontera, a Wisconsin-based immigrant rights organization. She found out that I was a teacher, participating in the march with my students, and she asked if I would say a few words to the press. I did and was quoted in the local newspaper, the Racine Journal Times.

It quickly became clear that Racine was not ready for this type of activity, nor for a teacher that would allow his students an opportunity to act in their interests in this way.

My comments created an uproar. The editorial page was filled with letters to the editor, slamming me and the "illegals." I used this as a teachable moment during class. I shared one of the more blatant anti-immigrant letters with the students. They were outraged. I asked them to critique the letter using a three-step process. First, I asked them to individually explain the author's main arguments to the editor. Second, I asked them to write down how the letter made them feel, and third, I asked them to evaluate their thinking to consider their own reasoned response to the letter.

In essence, I wanted them to counter the arguments being made. Then I wrote the same questions on the board and had students share what they were thinking. We reviewed the arguments and their brainstorming, and using their thoughts, we wrote letters to the editor. I told them I would submit them to the paper on their behalf. Many of the students volunteered to do so. The composed letters were excellent. I submitted them to the newspaper with a letter of explanation detailing how the letters came to be—the Journal Times printed my letter, as well as all of the uncensored and unedited student letters. In the piece, they included a large picture of the Statue of Liberty. The whole letter to the editor page was dedicated just to my students' responses.

The following letter, written by 10th grader Jessie Sanchez, is an excellent example of those that were published. In it, she said,

"This letter is in response to Mr. Peterson's letter to the editor. In his letter, he took issue with the immigrant labor rights protest. After reading Mr. Peterson's letter, our Latino-American History Class decided to respond. We believe his comments were unfair and very offensive. Mr. Peterson, all people on this planet, U.S. citizens or not, deserve justice and freedom. You say legal citizens do not have jobs because illegal immigrants

work for a much lower salary. It is not true. Illegal immigrants take jobs that most citizens do not want. Illegal immigrants benefit the economy by doing these jobs. They also pay taxes but do not receive benefits because they are not legal citizens... [this] doesn't mean they deserve to be treated less humanely than citizens. After all, doesn't our Pledge of Allegiance say, "Liberty and Justice for All"? Your comments made all of us feel very offended. Many of us are Hispanics and know people who are illegal. We understand how hard their lives are. They don't need nor deserve the types of comments you made. They are very hurtful. It made all of us feel upset, mad, and hurt. We hope that in the future you will either be more sensitive towards others or keep your comments to yourself. We hope our letter has given you something to think about."

After publishing my students' letters, there was an immediate backlash from racist, anti-immigrant community members. It fueled a running debate on immigration in Racine. This action was the beginning of connecting classroom learning with issues that mattered to the students, to their parents, and to the communities they were part of.

Shortly following the printing of the letters, the school hosted its annual parent open house. During this time, teachers spoke to parents in the classroom regarding what the students were learning.

My Latino History classroom was packed with parents. Every desk was filled. You could hear a pin drop when I spoke about the curriculum and my goal of connecting learning to the students' lives. A Hispanic gentleman raised his hands and asked why the emphasis was so heavily on immigration. I explained that while we covered many other issues, immigration was one of historical significance that affected many of our students' lives. It was clear he was not happy with my response, and from his tone, he appeared to be anti-immigrant. However, at the end of the classroom orientation, a group of parents came up to me and said they were proud that their sons or daughters wrote the letters. They asked me to continue the work I was doing. It struck me that the work we did on immigration connected the parents to their children in a meaningful way.

There were more parents that attended the Latino History class orientation than all of my other four classes combined.

My other classes had a mixture of Latino, African-American, and White students from poor and working-class families. The Latino turnout for the other classes was no greater than that of the Black or White parents.

It became obvious to me that if one's teaching is relevant to the students and their parents, they will respond. It was very exciting to see students advocating for themselves, for their parents, and for their communities. Parents were very proud of their children and the work we had done left both wanting more.

My next opportunity in connecting students to real-world learning followed a guest speaker's attendance in my class. Christine Neuman-Ortiz, Executive Director of Voces de la Frontera, came to speak to my class. That day, we welcomed in the students from Victor Moreno's bilingual English class as well. Victor Moreno was a very popular and beloved bilingual teacher.

Neuman-Ortiz's talk centered around the community organizing of Voces. The highlight of her presentation was discussion of lobbying work they were doing on in-state college tuition for undocumented students. She mentioned that the following day there would be a hearing on in-state tuition for undocumented students at the capitol in Madison.

I asked her if she would pay for a bus for my students to attend.

She replied, "Absolutely."

Latino-American History students on the steps of the state capitol. This picture was taken shortly after their testifying for in-state tuition for undocumented students
Photo by Allen Levie

"It was the first time that I spoke publicly. It was very, very scary. I remember my legs trembling like they were made of jelly. Afterward, I felt powerful and accomplished. I knew that I must continue speaking up and that I could make a difference."

Brenda Garcia

That was the beginning of the connection between my students and their community.

For that trip, Victor and I acted as chaperones. We escorted forty students to Madison. During the long bus trip, Victor and I worked with the students on their individual testimonies for the hearing. The students wrote them and we made edits. We had them practice their speeches with us first and then with one another. The ninety minutes flew by; there was a buzz in the air, a palpable excitement.

When we arrived at the hearing every student signed up to speak. The sponsor of the bill, Senator Pedro Colon, held a press conference outside the meeting room where the bill was being discussed. My students witnessed him speaking on the moral imperative of the passage of the bill. It was music to their ears. He was talking about many of them. Senator Colon was impressed that so many students came in support of the bill.

The public hearing started right after his press conference. After ending his comments to the press, he told us he appreciated our support, but that the meeting room was too small to accommodate them all. He suggested that we not go in. The students who heard his request were crestfallen. They had been fully engaged in putting together their testimonies and looked forward to presenting them.

Victor and I discounted his advice. Disappointing the kids was not an option. We hadn't come all that way for the kids to be shut out of the room. Victor led the students into the room and I pushed them from behind. They all fit, lining the walls of the beautiful meeting room, the likes of which was something they never imagined existed. Most were wide eyed in awe and scared at the same time.

Cecilia, a ninth grader, recounted, "Initially I was intimidated and nervous coming into that space. I didn't believe that they would listen. We were just a bunch of kids."

Speaker after speaker testified. Some for the proposed bill and some against it. Our time was running short, and our students had not yet had the opportunity to speak. The bus that brought the students to the capitol was soon scheduled to leave and bring us all back to Racine. It appeared that my students would not be able to present their excellent testimonies.

Victor, my fellow teacher, unsolicited, stood up and in his teacher's voice, said to the committee, "Excuse me, but these students (gesturing around the room) came from Racine Horlick High School to speak about this issue. They will be leaving soon, so will you please allow them to speak?"

The committee chair opened the floor to the students. They spoke eloquently about why undocumented students should receive in-state tuition. After one or two students spoke, the chair asked a student who was about to speak if she was undocumented. She froze, knowing that speaking could put her in danger. Another student, Brenda Garcia, who was standing in front of the packed room, turned to make eye contact with me and nodded her head as if to say, *I'll speak.*

I nodded back.

She squeezed her way to the microphone. This courageous fifteen-year-old student came forward, gently moving the other student to the side. In a clear and unshakable voice, she let the committee know why they should grant in-state tuition to her and others like her. She shared her status as an undocumented student. She advocated for those like her, sharing her dream of becoming a lawyer and her belief that she and all undocumented students have the right to follow their dreams. She testified that when legislators deny the right to an education, they are denying valuable resources to this country.

She said, "Who knows - it may be one of us, who, if given the opportunity, could develop a cure for cancer. Fulfilling our dreams isn't just about us, it's about the future of our country."

Brenda and I later spoke about the event, and she said, "It was the first time that I spoke publicly. It was very, very scary. I remember my legs trembling like they were made of jelly. Afterward, I felt powerful and accomplished. I knew that I must continue speaking up and that I could make a difference."

When Brenda boarded the bus home, the students erupted in thunderous applause for her. They recognized her courageous and eloquent effort. Brenda cried. What is significant about this experience for Brenda is that initially she was not liked by many of the first-generation Mexican-American students at Horlick. There existed in Horlick, as in other high schools, a division between undocumented immigrant students and the students born in the U.S. to undocumented parents.

According to Cecilia, "At that time, U.S.-born Mexican students hung out in one area of the building, and the immigrant students hung out in another area. Immigrant students felt that U.S.-born Mexicans felt they were better than them, and vice versa. The U.S.-born Mexicans felt that the immigrant students felt they were better."

There was a cultural divide.

Undocumented students were on the lowest scale of the social hierarchy in the school. The first-generation students distanced themselves from undocumented students.

Cecilia went on to say, "I think the in-state tuition struggle was something that definitely brought us together. We realized that we had more in common. We all wanted the same thing."

In the courageous act of standing up and representing herself, her family, and her classmates, an often troubled and belligerent teenager transformed into a confident and well-spoken young woman. I was very proud of Brenda that day. Brenda told me that the experience changed her. She said that before speaking that day, she was quite shy, struggling to present in front of her classmates. Coming forward and speaking up gave her the confidence to become a well-spoken student and immigrant rights leader.

Brenda said her mother, who had always told her to keep her head down and cautioned her not to draw attention to herself, as most immigrant parents do, now supported her. She saw a marked change in Brenda as a result of her involvement.

Brenda told me, "Keeping my head down took away my power and gave more power to my oppressors. I began to realize [that] the more I stood up, the more powerful and accomplished I became."

Upon reflection, I've been left with a sense of fulfillment, knowing that as her teacher I facilitated an opportunity for her growth.

Victor's role in the field trip was astounding. Initially, for him, it was an educational opportunity for "Hispanic" students to simply see and experience the Capitol.

Victor recently told me, "[For me] ...it was a way of getting the kids out of school to see the capital. It was your event, and I agreed to come along to make sure the kids were well-spoken."

I use the word "Hispanic" here in my recounting of Victor as distinct from Latino/a because it is the preferred term used by establishment-minded conservative Mexicans. Victor was very much an establishment Hispanic. He was the first Hispanic person to get a teaching job at Horlick for many years. He created the school's bilingual program. Before he arrived, there were only five to ten Hispanic students in the bilingual program out of an enrollment of over 200. He hooked the students into taking his class by establishing clubs and activities that spoke to and related to them.

The bilingual students came to realize that he cared about them, and they began to flock to his classes. Victor's interaction with the students went beyond the classroom. He would train students to become good employees and bring the most promising upwardly mobile Latino students regularly to the Hispanic business roundtable luncheons. Yearly, he took a busload of students to the baseball game to watch the Milwaukee Brewers play. Victor coached and trained the girls in Latin dance. They performed at the student assemblies. Victor started many Hispanic sports leagues. He did his best to provide positive experiences for the Latino population at Horlick.

However, Victor's interaction with those students on that day of lobbying in Madison changed him. His preparing students to testify, his pushing his way into the hearing with the students, and his standing up for them before the committee chair to ensure that their voices were heard all left their mark on him.

Recently, when I pointed out that interrupting the committee proceedings that day was out of character for him, he responded, "I don't know what came over me. I just had to say it. Those kids came for a purpose, and they had to be heard."

As a result of Victor's actions, his credibility as a role model to the students and their respect for him increased. Victor stood up for them, and they did not forget it.

As an educator, I believed that the action in Madison was totally aligned with a service-learning approach to education, involving students in community projects and activities related to the curriculum. After the field trip, I began to see mediocre and disinterested students in my class start to take learning seriously, focusing more on learning and less on fooling around in class. The connection that we made between the class and their lives was beginning to have an effect. My classroom projects and activities were designed to encourage students to take action on issues of importance.

One such activity, the immigrant interviews, had a profound impact on students' desire to create positive change. I always included immigrant interviews as a culminating activity in our study on immigration. The students were to interview anyone they knew who came from another country. It could be a family member, friend, or member of the community. If they didn't have anyone to connect with, I helped set up interviews for them. The vast majority, however, had no problem finding someone to interview. The students were given eight primary questions to ask, questions that struck at the heart of the immigration experience:

- Where do you come from?
- What was it like there?
- Why did you leave?
- Describe the journey.
- Why did you choose Racine?
- What was life like when you got here?
- What obstacles did you face?
- Is life here as you expected it would be?

We would simulate an interview in class, and I instructed the students not to take notes when they interviewed people. They were simply to listen intently - to make it conversational. After the interview they were to write up a one-to-two-page reflection on the interview, summarizing the responses and the interaction between them and the person they interviewed. They then were asked to reflect on what they learned and how they felt about it. The final part of the project involved presentations of the interviews to the whole class. They could review their notes or reflection paper during their presentations, but the process was more conversational and questions from the other students were encouraged. Throughout the years, the results were phenomenal. Many students connected with their parents in an extremely meaningful way. Very few parents had spoken to their children about their own immigrant experience. Many cried while telling their stories. The students grew immensely as a result of the project. Ruby, a very self-assured freshman, started to tear up as she began her presentation. This reaction was out of character for Ruby, as her strongest suit had always been her confidence. I stopped Ruby's presentation and brought another student forward to continue in her place. It was clear Ruby was getting ready to cry. I told her she could just hand in her notes and her report. The next day, Ruby apologized for her presentation and said she was ready to try again. She spoke about her mother's immigration experience, about how she was pregnant with her older sister when she crossed the border. She was transported in a cargo van. Her mom told her that they were in the locked bed of that van for hours. It was so hot she feared for her life. At one point the van stopped and they were told to be quiet. Ruby's mother feared that the drivers would run off and leave them. It is no wonder that Ruby had a tough time retelling the story. She said that just thinking about it the previous day had brought her to tears. The experience of telling her mother's story was cathartic for her.

The classroom took on a workshop ambiance. While students shared experiences, classmates gave support or asked clarifying questions. The experience cemented a collective understanding of what it meant to immigrate and the obstacles that their parents, friends and community members faced. These interviews developed a resolve in the students, cementing in them the desire to stand up for justice for immigrants. The students and their parents were brought closer together.

Together, students were sparked into taking action for themselves, their families, and their friends.

CHAPTER 3
EMERGING STUDENT ACTIVISM

Horlick Latino-American history class students participating in Dream Act mock graduation ceremony in Washington, D.C.
Photo by Jennifer Levie

Classroom learning, coupled with participation in relevant community activity and action around issues that mattered to them promoted emerging student activism.

The student trip to Madison in support of in-state tuition laid the foundation for our annual Washington D.C. excursion. This trip to Washington D.C. trained emerging student leaders and began a long and prosperous relationship between Voces de La Frontera, a statewide immigrant rights group, and the Latino youth at Horlick High School. Clearly, the students' presence and their eloquent presentations at the Capitol impressed Voces leadership.

Shortly after the trip to Madison, I spoke with Christine Neuman

Ortiz, Executive Director of the organization, and asked her if there were any other activities that my students could be involved in. She said there was an approaching day of action in Washington, D.C to draw attention to the *Dream Act*, the proposed bill to give undocumented youth a pathway to citizenship. I asked Christine if Voces would be willing to fund a group of Horlick students and myself to participate in the activities. She agreed to do so. In class, we studied the components of the *Dream Act*. Students were then offered an opportunity to attend the event in Washington. I let them know we could take eight students, and that all expenses would be paid. I created an application and timeline for completion. As part of the application, students had to write a one-page essay in Spanish or in English on the meaning of the *Dream Act* and on its importance to undocumented youth. They also had to provide a rationale for why they wanted to participate in the trip. As it turned out, only 9 students applied, and one of the applicants turned in their application late, resulting in all eight students attending.

The trip to Washington was memorable. I, along with my wife, 2-year-old son, and Maria Morales, a long-time civil rights and immigrant advocate, chaperoned the students. In subsequent conversation with Maria, she said, *"...I decided to go on the trip out of concern [that] some of the immigrant parents had expressed regarding allowing their children to go on this type of trip. My going was reassuring to the parents that their kids would be ok."*

The majority of the students on the trip were rough around the edges, lively kids. None had been to Washington, D.C. before. Most had never been on an airplane. I sat next to one of my students who was scared of flying. When the plane took off, tears began rolling down her cheeks. When we got off the plane in Washington, I sat them down and reiterated the rules of the trip. We had to take the underground metro from the airport to where we were staying. I told them if we got separated, we would all get off and wait at the next stop. These street-smart Racine kids said, almost in unison, *"No one is going to be left behind."* They were petrified at the possibility. One of the students wanted to know if we were going to have a chance to go to the mall. Yes, I replied. We were going to the largest mall in the world. They all cheered and wanted to know when. I told them as soon as we dropped off our luggage and had a little lunch we would head over there. They were very excited. As promised, we dropped off our luggage, had lunch, and then caught the Metro to the mall. They were shocked when we reached the mall. It was not at all the kind of mall they expected. It was the National Mall. It took them no time at all to pivot. They were enthralled with the great museums and government buildings. We spent two days walking around the Mall, seeing the sights. The museum that impressed them the most was the Holocaust Museum. Immersed in the experience, they walked in silence, moving at their own pace. I promised the students that after we finished the museum, we would go to the shopping mall. Seven of the eight students finished in an hour and a half. Laura Agurrie, however, was so caught up in the exhibit that she was still inside after three hours. The other students became extremely agitated, wanting to know where Laura was. I was forced to go back in and found her studying the railroad cars used to transport people to the death camps. She was clearly moved by the experience. Her parents were from El Salvador. When she and I came out of the exhibit we were greeted by some mildly agitated students. However, they all had been affected by the museum, so they weren't too hard on Laura.

The *Dream Act* day of action at the Capitol provided the motivation and education that I had hoped for. It had actually begun the day before, with a discussion by around 100 students from mostly all over the East Coast to plan out the day's action. My students were blown away at the level of discussion, and more importantly, by the diversity of the immigrant population in attendance. They themselves were mostly of Mexican descent or from Mexico. The immigrants they came in contact with were from Africa, Asia, and Europe, with some from Central and South America. It was an eye-opening experience for them. Seeing kids from all around the world, working together to improve their situation, gave my students something to think about.

At the main press conference the next day, along with the others, Horlick students were dressed in graduation caps and gowns. They were interviewed by a Washington Post reporter and their picture appeared on the front page the next day. Horlick students were quoted in the article about the experience, providing testimonials as to why they were there participating. It was a real confidence booster for them. What they had to say had value.

The Washington D.C. trip, sponsored by Voces de la Frontera was the first in a series of yearly political education and lobbying trips to Washington that spanned over 12 years. These trips expanded my students' understanding of the world and exposed them to institutions and individuals that gave them the tools to act.

BACKLASH FROM WASHINGTON TRIP AND COMMUNITY RESPONSE

Parents, students and community members coming to my defense
Photo by Steve Avila

The trip to Washington D.C. changed the students. They were now motivated to organize around fair and humane immigration reform. It garnered a lot of media attention from the local press in both Racine and Milwaukee. A local anti-immigrant community member came to the Racine Unified School Board and asked for my resignation. She said that R.U.S.D. teachers had no business promoting illegal activity. I received a call the very next day from the Deputy Superintendent, who said he was calling on behalf of the R.U.S.D. School Board. He told me that a community member had raised issues with the trip and that he wanted me to spell out the particulars of it. This request was made despite the fact that prior to the approval of the trip, I had detailed in the field trip request form exactly what we would be doing in Washington and the school board had approved the trip. Being called by the Deputy Superintendent raised concerns. Was the school board going to attempt to sanction me?

I immediately got on the phone with Maria Morales, who had accompanied us on the trip, and discussed the situation with her. We strategized what to do next. It was decided that the next school board meeting needed to have a parent, student and community presence. Maria organized the students, their parents and various community members to come to the school board meeting in support of me and of the trip. Approximately 50 people came and stood in solidarity with us. Parents and the students who went to Washington D.C. spoke at the school board meeting. They thanked the school board for approving the trip and emphasized what a wonderful experience it was. No one mentioned my name. Any talk of dismissing me, however, ended before it started.

Clearly, if there had not been a public response, I would have been disciplined in some way, and my attempts to build student power at Horlick would have been short-lived.

The students, their parents and the community felt their power that day. They knew that they were standing up for and supporting a teacher who was teaching history in a way that spoke to their lives.

SEPTEMBER 16TH CELEBRATION

Horlick Principal Nola Ratliff doing a Mexican line dance at Fiesta Patria Photo Al Levie

After the school board meeting, the students and I met and debriefed about what took place at the school board meeting. The students decided they needed to continue to organize support for the *Dream Act*. They planned a September 16th celebration to garner student and community support. They built a sizable following and base of supporters that would ensure a successful event. The participation of the students in the immigrant tour, their letters to the editor, the trips to Madison and Washington D.C. for in-state tuition and the *Dream Act*, their public defense of their teacher, and their legitimate right to lobby on issues they found important all contributed to the smashing success of the event. They worked hard to organize the celebration. The recognition from fellow students, parents, friends and the community contributed to a massive turnout and a successful program. Over 500 students, parents and community members attended. It was stellar. Horlick's principal welcomed everyone in both English and Spanish. There was an all-star lineup of prominent Latino leaders. Dr. Jose Martinez, the new Latino Deputy Superintendent in Racine Unified MCed the event. The keynote speaker was a prominent Latino activist, Jesus Salas. He was well known throughout the state for his organizing efforts in helping farm workers secure basic human rights in the fields. He was a professor at a local college. Christine Neuman Ortiz, Director of Voces de La Frontera, spoke about the current state of immigrant rights organizing both nationally and in the state.

Most importantly, the students who had taken the trip to Washington D.C. both spoke and played an organizing role at the event. They created the decorations, greeted people as they came in and oversaw the logistical aspects of the event. In addition, they eloquently spoke about their trip and its impact on them and the importance of the *Dream Act*. There was full support for the event. Maria Morales played an important role as well. Both she and the students contacted local Mexican restaurants and stores to secure food and drink donations. It was by far the largest Latino sponsored event the school had ever held. It uplifted the Latino community, showing great care for the community and support for the students in their efforts.

It marked the beginning of Horlick and its students' role at the center of immigrant rights organizing in Racine. The students were developing self-confidence and a sense of purpose.

Following this event, the emerging student activists decided to start a student group that would focus on organizing for immigrant issues. They met in my room and decided on the name "Students United For Immigrant Rights". They created an acronym and called themselves S.U.F.R.I.R. They added the extra "R" because "sufrir" in Spanish means "to suffer". They felt the name spoke to the suffering and plight of immigrant students.

The students and I met with Horlick Principal Nola Starling-Ratliff to hear what steps were needed in order to make S.U.F.R.I.R an official club. She was at first reluctant to accept the new group, but nervously, she went along with it. It was a student-driven group made up of an oppressed minority; there was no choice but to accept it. She herself, as the first African-American woman principal at the school, often had to walk a fine line. Although she supported the kids, I recently interviewed her and asked why there was hesitation on her part in accepting the student activist clubs.

She said, *"It wasn't hesitation on my part as much as hesitation on the district's part. Let's say it that way politically. We have to stay out of politics as such, and when you move into the political arena that is where you draw the line. We could do what we needed to do in our building. But when you went outside of the building and into the community, everybody was seeing it."*

Essentially, Nola was correct in her assessment. Establishing a club that promoted students working on real issues that affected them, their parents and their communities and linking up with community partners was frowned on by the administrators in the school district. Their policies were designed to avoid controversy and maintain the status quo – a status quo that did not serve minority students.

I give Starling-Ratliff credit for not trying to stop S.U.F.R.I.R's formation as a school-based club.

CHAPTER 4
ORGANIZING FOR POWER

A mock graduation on the steps of Horlick dramatizing the need for in-state tuition for undocumented students
Photo by Allen Levie

"I have cousins who are undocumented and will never be able to afford college if they pay out of state tuition"

LOUISA MORELOS

S.U.F.R.I.R. played a significant role in building momentum for the eventual passage of a bill in the state legislature that extended in-state tuition to Wisconsin undocumented residents.

S.U.F.R.I.R's first action was to hold a mock graduation on the front steps of the school. Immigrant and non-immigrant students and community supporters lined the steps of the school with signs that asked, "What's next?" A press conference included local politicians, students, teachers and community members speaking in support of the bill that was before the state legislature which would grant in-state tuition to undocumented students. S.U.F.R.I.R student Estella Cabrerra MCed the event. The speakers were inspiring. Around 200 students either participated or watched. The event was captured by the local media.

S.U.F.R.I.R was now an established entity in the school and in the community. It had gained club status in the school and tied itself to Voces de la Frontera as its youth organizing arm. Voces played an important role in the development of S.U.F.R.I.R. It brought valuable resources to S.U.F.R.I.R., including money for leadership development, field trips and issue development. The students and I were given a place on the Voces statewide steering committee, which assisted in developing the issue campaigns for Voces and acted as an oversight body on financial and organizational matters. Voces valued student participation and put them front and center in all of their major actions.

Teaching from a social justice perspective facilitated student empowerment. It promoted authentic student learning, leading to the kind of self-awareness and confidence that helped students make positive changes in their lives and in their communities.

The movie *Walk Out* was a phenomenal teaching tool. Studying it with the students helped them understand that change never comes easy, and that in order to create it, one has to be organized. The movie is about the Los Angeles Chicano high school student walkouts, organized to demand better treatment and opportunities in the schools. It stimulated many discussions for the students in my classes and in S.U.F.R.I.R about how the youth got organized, what their campaigns looked like, what choices they made in dealing with obstacles and why they won. The students wrote 3-to-5-page papers about the L.A. walkouts and how it applied to their lives.

The inclusion of this movie in the study of the Chicano movement helped Horlick students develop a frame for understanding their issues. It acted as a catalyst to action.

Below are a few of the many examples of students building power in their school:

Ash Wednesday

Maria Morales approached me on behalf of the religious community to have Horlick S.U.F.R.I.R. host an Ash Wednesday event on the front steps of Horlick High School in order to dramatize the sacrifices made by immigrant families coming to the United States. Horlick Students, staff, and local community activists and religious leaders all spoke about the dangers and hardships faced by undocumented families during their journeys to cross the border. Coffins and signs were used to symbolize that sacrifice.

Ash Wednesday event at Horlick dramatizing
the need for immigration reform
Photo by Al Levie

"My stepfather had just been deported and not allowed to return for 10 years. Our family situation was not good. It felt really good having all those people there. Some who were there were in similar family situations and some were not. There were all kinds of people coming together to support immigrants. It felt really comforting."

Jose Sanchez

Jose was representative of many of the students who attended the event. They felt supported and valued at a time in their life when it was most needed. Staff, fellow students as well as church and community leaders all came and showed their support for the immigrant youth and the hardships their families faced.

Ash Wednesday Event
Photo by Al Levie

Park and Ride Mock Graduation

In 2004, in an effort to highlight the hypocrisy of President Bush's commencement speech at Concordia University in Mequon, Wisconsin after his refusal to pass pro-immigration legislation that would provide undocumented students with a pathway to college, students and community members organized a mock graduation event. These students and people in the community saw this as an opportunity to highlight the plight of undocumented immigrant students who had no access to student aid and had limited opportunities, even with a college diploma.

The event was energizing. It strengthened the student and community bond that was developing among immigrant students. Voces de La Frontera and the S.U.F.R.I.R students decided to host a mock graduation to highlight the plight of immigrant students. It was held at a park and ride lot at the same time that President Bush was giving a commencement speech at a private college on the north side of Milwaukee. Two school bus loads full of SUFRIR students participated, around 80 students total. Many were undocumented. It was raining that day, and the adult participants were skeptical that it would go as planned. It rained so hard you could barely see your hand in front of your face. Several students came to the rescue. They climbed on top of the buses and secured tarps between them, providing a canopy to shield the participants. Jon, an undocumented student, told me, *"We just did what we had to do."*

It was a beautiful ceremony. Prominent community leaders and students spoke.

All of the adults present, myself included, were in awe of these high school students. They rose to the occasion. Some of the very students that teachers complained about not being engaged in their lessons were engaged in this event; they were invested and passionate.

Passive learners became active participants.

Louisa Morelos, S.U.F.R.I.R student speaking at MATC
Photo by Jennifer Levie

S.U.F.R.I.R responds to racist comments by talk radio host Mark Belling

Above is a photo of Louisa, a S.U.F.R.I.R student speaking at Milwaukee Area Technical College board meeting on behalf of the organization. The meeting dealt with the removal of advertising dollars from a local radio station because of the racist comments made on the air by Mark Belling, a prominent right wing radio personality. Louisa is reading from the text of a commentary that she had published in the Racine Journal Times.

"Before election day, me and my friends knew that there was a good chance that the district would cancel the field trip. We had already decided that we were going to do it if they did. It was about our community and building power."

XAVIER MARQUEZ

Student Election Day Get Out The Vote

Students in S.U.F.R.I.R started to realize that if their communities were going to be heard and accounted for, they needed to increase voter turnout. Traditionally, Latinos in Racine lived in the wards with the lowest voter turnout. Voces De La Frontera organized the first ever Get Out the Vote (G.O.T.V.) event in the city of Racine in 2004. This activity created a major political shift at Horlick. On behalf of S.U.F.R.I.R, I put in for a field trip with my department chair to do an Election Day Get Out The Vote effort with Horlick students. The idea was that students would go door to door and encourage city residents to vote. My department chair denied the request. He said that it didn't fit into his traditional definition of a field trip. Clearly, he was not ready for this type of service-learning project. He didn't feel that it aligned with the social studies curriculum. At one point he said that he himself had never knocked on doors, essentially arguing that it was not a necessary civic engagement project. Once again, I went over his head and convinced the Assistant Superintendent to support the project. My department chair pushed back, raising arguments that centered around child safety and organization. Rather than deny the field trip request, the Assistant Superintendent assigned the department chair to work with me on the project in order to ensure that it went smoothly and that student safety issues were addressed. My department chair met with me one time to hear the plan and after that, distanced himself from it altogether.

Students, however, participated at every level of the planning and execution of the Get Out The Vote project.

S.U.F.R.I.R student leaders organized a G.O.T.V steering committee. The committee consisted of Dick Kinch, a longtime peace activist in the community, Father Bruce Clanton, a Catholic Priest who worked with alienated youth, Beverly Hicks, President of the NAACP as well as Horlick teachers and student members of S.U.F.R.I.R. Several planning meetings took place to ensure that it would be a successful event.

The plan crystallized into an organized system for ensuring that all 33 voting wards in the city would be canvassed. The canvass headquarters was to be Memorial Hall in downtown Racine. Ryan, an English as a Second Language teacher, secured the maps and developed routes for buses. Students, other teachers and myself developed instructional materials, designed non-partisan literature and recruited students and adult chaperones for the effort. Buses were to pick up students and transport them to and from their assigned wards. Student and adult participants were to be given bright, neon t-shirts, clearly identifying them as participants. All 300 students were to be transported back to Memorial Hall for lunch where students would be fed, served pizza and snacks. During the afternoon break, there was to be a brief educational program, in which canvassing stories were to be shared. Afterwards, students and adult chaperones were to be picked up and transported back to their wards to continue canvassing efforts. This massive organizational effort was part of the statewide G.O.T.V. push headed by Voces de La Frontera, who funded the cost of the event.

Ultimately, the school board approved the field trip canvas. Over 300 students were recruited to participate in the effort alongside adult chaperones, comprised of both teachers and community members.

Everything seemed to be all set.

But it was not.

The local media covering the school board meeting at which the field trip was approved became interested in the event and gave it extensive coverage. People For The American Way, a right-wing group, as well as right-leaning media outlets, began beating the drum that the G.O.T.V was a partisan effort. The areas being canvassed, they warned, traditionally voted democratic. Therefore, they argued that it should not take place at all. It became statewide and national news. The extremely tight 2004 presidential election of George Bush versus John Kerry was at stake, and they feared Racine could turn the election in Wisconsin for Kerry.

Two weeks before the election I told Jen, my wife, that the school board might cancel the field trip. She asked, *"What will you do?"* I told her that I wanted to do it anyway, and if I did it might result in me getting fired. She told me that no matter what, we would be fine, that we would go to "Plan B". When I asked her what Plan B was, she said that she didn't know, but that together, we would figure it out. My wife's response was courageous. Our son was 2 years old, and she was a stay-at-home mom. Losing the job would certainly have disrupted our lives.

Sure enough, the day before the election, I received a call from Dr. Martinez, the RUSD Deputy Superintendent. He told me that the school board had canceled the field trip. I told him that that was fine, but that we were going to do it anyway. His response revealed his panic. He said, *"You can't, it will appear that the district supports the G.O.T.V."* I told him that it was my civic right to take off on election day and work on the election. I asked him if I would still have a job on November 5th. He said yes. He then asked, for the sake of the district, if I could keep a low profile. I told him absolutely not. The district's cancellation of the field trip meant that none of the teacher chaperones would be participating. They were all new teachers and could not afford to take an unpaid day nor would they want to be seen in a bad light by the district. It dictated that I would have to be very visible.

Immediately after the call, Mark Zanin, a Horlick sub school principal, approached me and directed me to make an announcement canceling the field trip. I told him no. I told him that if he wanted to make an announcement he could. Xavier Marquez, President of S.U.F.R.I.R at the time, happened to overhear this exchange, and said that he would make the announcement. Xavier and Mr. Zanin went to his office and crafted an announcement that Xavier was going to read at the end of the day.

What happened next was significant. Xavier took the paper with the script he had written with Mr. Zahn and threw it into the wastebasket. He got on the loudspeaker in the main office and said, *"Hi, this is Xavier Marquez, President of Students United for Immigrant Rights. The district has dropped its support for our Get Out The Vote but we are going to do it anyhow. If you want to participate the buses will be loading on the street behind Horlick. If you want to meet us, we will be at Memorial Hall at 8:00 am."*

I recently asked Xavier why he changed the announcement. He said, *"...before election day, me and my friends knew that there was a good chance that the district would cancel the field trip. We had already decided that we were going to do it if they did. It was about our community and building power."*

The next day, Dick Kinch and I, along with a few other adults, were at Memorial Hall. There were 32 round tables, each with

10 chairs around them set up for the adult chaperones. To my recollection, it was a cold and dreary morning. There was a mist that hung in the air. I didn't believe the students would come. I asked Dick what we should do. He told me to set up the materials and just *"... see what happens"*. I was nervous, but that ultimately proved pointless. At 8:45 AM, buses full of kids arrived. Every table was filled. Over 250 Horlick students showed up that day. They looked determined, fierce. They were a real cross section of the school's student population: African American, Latino, White, working and middle class. It was quite a sight. Community volunteers served students a light breakfast as the S.U.F.R.I.R. students kicked into high gear. The students at each table immediately began putting polling location labels on the door literature. Others began to prepare for the kick-off program, which consisted of students explaining what was going to happen that day. Community members and students alike explained the importance of what they were doing that day. They gave instructions for canvassing, which included role playing by students on door-to-door canvassing and safety protocols.

The highlight of the morning event was when a small working class White girl, Kristina Folk, unsolicited, got up on stage and very eloquently read from a statement she had prepared on the importance of what they were doing and why she decided to come out that day. Her voice shook, but her words were mighty. Recently, Kristina told me, *"I was really scared to get up and speak. I had never spoken in public before, but I just felt like it was wrong for the district to take this opportunity away from us and that what we were about to do was really important. After the speech, I was ready to go. I felt powerful. My speaking that day has helped me to feel confident when I speak to large numbers of people. I am now a manager at Olive Garden and I often have to speak to up to 100 employees. When I go by the neighborhood, I canvassed it brings back good memories."*

The day was a resounding success; it went off without a hitch. Students knocked on over 25,000 doors without incident. They had a great day outside of school, participating in a meaningful, real-world activity that connected their education to their lives - the definition of social studies.

What happened afterward was even more significant than the day itself. I received countless letters in my school mailbox, thanking me for the opportunity to participate in the event. Some students, fearing for my job, went so far as to tell me that I had nothing to fear, that they had my back.

The most revealing consequence, however, came during the debriefing. Students retold how they had doors slammed in their face by people hostile to their efforts. One student talked about a homeowner's dog chasing her down the block. The stories were rich and colorful, full of life. Clearly, they were proud of what they had accomplished and were not daunted by those that opposed their efforts; rather, they were strengthened through their collective experience. They very powerfully handled contrary adults. They reversed roles. The most powerful testimony happened during a debriefing in my junior sociology class. It came from a Latina girl who rarely participated in the class. She sat in the back of the room and by choice had largely been invisible for most of the year. She said, *"Mr. Levie, everything changed as a result of yesterday. We gained power and we are never going to give it back."* A hush fell over the classroom. Many of the students sat quietly, solemnly but powerfully, and nodded their heads in agreement.

That first successful G.O.T.V. was a game changer.

On a personal level, this event was extremely important to my development. At the time, I believed that if I did not follow through with the G.O.T.V., I would be a hypocrite.

I believed then, as I believe now, that if you are to make changes in the world, you must be willing to take risks.

There is no other way to challenge the status quo. It was a definite risk to tell the school district that I was going to lead the Get Out The Vote, with or without their support. But it was equally as validating to see so many students standing up and doing what they thought was right, despite possible repercussions.

On a political level, the act of supporting the students and doing the G.O.T.V was important. It showed the students that a teacher would put their job on the line for them. It cemented our relationship and assured them that they would not be abandoned if they chose to take action.

On a community level, the G.O.T.V. campaign was very significant. Parents and community activists began to see the students as a political force within their community. As a result, community organizations began to invite S.U.F.R.I.R to their events.

Within the school, working class and poor students began to feel their power. They had never before been a driving force for change in this way, but the effort elevated their status. Other students took notice of their bold, controversial actions and lent their support.

Incidentally, Estelle, a S.U.F.R.I.R. student leader who helped organize the event, told me that on the morning of the G.O.T.V. effort, over two hundred students were ushered into the auditorium at Horlick High School and were prevented from participating. She was one of them. This brought the total number of participants to 500 - almost one-fourth of the student body of Horlick. Of those who participated in the event, one-third were Latino, one-third were African American, and one-third were White. They came from all the economic groupings within the school. What further added to the significance was that the leadership was mostly immigrant and first-generation Latino students, a group that was generally voiceless at the school.

Additionally, educators at the school stood up and took notice. Days before the event, as the controversy was building, many teachers expressed not only concern but opposition. Some said it was unsafe for the students to be walking in those neighborhoods. But the majority of students were *from* those very neighborhoods or walked through them on their way to school. Among some, there was a feeling that by participating in the G.O.T.V. as a teacher I was tarnishing the reputation of the rest. One social studies teacher told me quite directly that it was teachers like me that gave teachers a bad name, and that I was using the kids to push my own political agenda.

Incidentally, none of the teachers who had volunteered to participate followed through on their commitment that day.

However, some had been very active in helping plan the day. Ryan Knudson, a teacher who played an invaluable role in creating the walking routes and coordinating the bus drop off and pick up spots, came to Memorial Hall after school on the day of the event. He looked around the space. Even though the kids were gone, you could still feel their presence. I could tell that he wished he could have participated. He said he really wanted to attend, but that his students needed him. He went on to say that he couldn't risk getting fired. Ryan chose to play it safe that day. I told him that it was a great day, and that I, too, had feared what might happen to me as a teacher, but sometimes you just have to take the risk.

This was just the first of many G.O.T.V. efforts. The student activists at Horlick organized these massive Election Day door-to-door turn out activities for almost every significant local, state, and national election day. For future G.O.T.V. efforts we did not seek school district approval. Students simply had their parents call the attendance clerks and tell them that their child was attending a community event, thereby making it an excused absence. Our school district had a policy where parents could call their children out of school on an excused absence in order to take part in family activities. For some, it was to excuse students for deer hunting season.

For us, it was all about election season or participation in community events.

Beginnings of Black/Brown UNITY

Latino students were fully engaging in the work of S.U.F.R.I.R. They were making a name for themselves in the school and in the community. They were quoted in and wrote guest editorials to the local newspapers and planned and led major events supporting immigration reform and the *Dream Act*.

At the same time, another group of students began to emerge in defense of immigrant rights, and that was the African American students, many of whom were in my African American History classes. They, too, began to participate in marches and other activities in defense of the immigrant students.

I remember a particularly memorable experience. The students, along with Voces adults and parents, had a lobby day at the state capitol in Madison. One of the major issues that day was in-state tuition for undocumented students. The Republicans, knowing when we were coming to Madison, chose to go into a closed-door caucus. When the students found out they were enraged. They charged into the room. The Republican Chair told the students that if they didn't leave, they would be arrested. LaRonda, an African American student, said to the Republican lawmakers, with tears streaming down her face, *"You are wrong. We fought for our rights to have a decent education, and you have no right to deny those students the right to a college education."*

The level of solidarity between black and brown students was growing. There had previously been a clear divide between the two, but it was rapidly dissipating.

Students organize successful King Day events
Photo by Al Levie

Black Students Organize

Brandon Tolliver, Laqueta Barker, and Kamala Richardson were three of the African American students who participated in the Madison lobby day. Shortly thereafter, they came to my room after school and asked if I would support them as I had the Latino students. They wanted help organizing a Black student group in order to deal with their issues. I agreed. Clearly, the African American students wanted to find their voice, and it needed to be heard.

The timing was perfect, in that the groundwork for organizing for student agency and voice had already begun.

The establishment of Students United in the Struggle (S.U.I.T.S) was organic. Without a doubt, the most important prerequisite for me to be able to successfully facilitate the organization of an African American student group that served to build agency among them was trust. I had clearly gained that trust.

The story I am about to tell illustrates that trust between us.

Six years into working at Horlick, an inner-city school in Racine, Wisconsin, a depressed city with the second highest unemployment rate in the state, I was eating lunch in the Social Studies office, and teachers started to trickle in on their break. It dawned on me that something was wrong. The teachers coming in were not the teachers I normally had lunch with. I asked one of the teachers what hour it was. She replied, *"4th hour"*. I panicked; my lunch hour was during 5th period. I somehow got it in my mind that it was my lunch hour. During 4th hour, I taught African American History. Twenty minutes into the period, I dashed off to my classroom, very late. When I got there all the lights were off and the door was locked. I knocked on the door and a student in a low voice replied, *"Who is it?"* I said, *"It's Mr. Levie"*. He came to the door and opened it. All of the students were sitting at their desks in the dark with their heads down. I asked what they were doing. One simply replied, *"We got your back, Mr. Levie."*

The groundwork for the establishment of S.U.I.T.S started in my African American History classroom. The students learned what they already felt - that they were oppressed and that the system was rigged against them. In that class, I created a framework for them, one that helped them understand their oppression as well as a way for them to overcome it.

The lessons I taught reinforced what they already knew.

I taught about the development of racism as a system of oppression and how it has been institutionalized in America. They learned about their peoples' struggles to overcome the racist and classist nature of their oppression. I taught the movie *The Children's March*, a video produced by the Southern Poverty Law Center, a group dedicated to fighting for Racial Justice, showed how students protesting in Birmingham stood up to the racist city establishment and ultimately won. I showed this video to my students in African American History. Many lessons were geared toward developing an understanding of how the system oppressed African Americans and how the students of Birmingham brought the racist system to its knees. The students we studied were responsible for ending the Jim Crow practices that kept African Americans from enjoying the same privileges as their white counterparts.

The Great Migration interview project, much like the Latino Immigration project, allowed students to connect with their elders. It opened the door to creating conversations that built investment in both themselves and their families. They gained insight into their ancestors' stories, learning about why they left the south and what they found when they came here. Like their Latino brothers and sisters, as a result of hearing and retelling those stories, they began caring more deeply about themselves and about one another. And from that care was born the spark that lit their enthusiasm for activism both in their school and in their community.

In my courses, classroom activities and student activism were fundamentally linked. In My African American History class, one such activity involved collective response to a racist comment made in our community.

Racine Alderman Engels, while chairing a public meeting, made a racist jab as a joke at a black community activist after he exceeded a three-minute time limit for public testimony. Mr. Engels stated to the community member, *"My watch has a black face"*, and *"... this is not a prejudiced watch"*. This incident was reported on by the Racine Journal Times on September 14, 2004. I shared this story with the students in my African American History classes. Similarly, as I had done with the students in the Latino American History class, I asked them if they would like to respond to the comments. Overwhelmingly they said yes. So, I asked each of them to write how they felt about Mr. Engel's comments, and to write what they would say to him if they were given a chance. I then asked them to write their collective wisdom on the chalkboard. Afterwards, I asked for volunteers to write letters based on their responses. They articulately shared their perspective. I sent both a letter of explanation and the students' work to the Racine Journal Times, asking them to print the letters. Not only did they print all of the students' letters and my letter of explanation, but they included a drawing that depicted a white and black silhouette touching a body of land.

Here is an example of one of the letters published:

Comment Uncalled For

I feel that Ald. Thomas Engel's comment was completely uncalled for. The situation could have been handled in a much better way. Engel could have simply told Alphonso Gardener that he timed him and he exceeded three minutes. I believe it is very important and necessary that Engel apologizes to the Black community, not only because he's white and made a racist comment, which offended African Americans, but he's part of the City Council and makes decisions for rights and jobs in our community. Engel may not be prejudiced, but his statement implies that he is, and I wouldn't want a person prejudiced against any race on City Council. So, if he says he is not prejudiced, then an apology needs to be made. I ask Engel to picture himself in a situation where a comment or joke is made referring to or making fun of his race by anyone who is an elected official who makes decisions for our country, state, or city. How would he feel? Wouldn't he demand an apology?

Briana King
Horlick High School

Group picture in front of Chicago's DuSable
Museum of African-American History
PHOTO BY AL LEVIE

Another significant activity in my African American History class was an annual trip to the Chicago DuSable Museum of African American History. It included lunch at Pearl's, a soul food restaurant in Chicago. This was an all-day field trip. I made sure that it was free to the students. The cost of the bus came out of the school budget, but the cost of a meal at Pearl's was provided as a gift by the daughter of Ms. Ratliff, the school's principal.

Students pose at Pearl's in Chicago
Photo by Al Levie

Student performers applaud the 250 people in the audience for coming and encouraged them to stay for the soul food dinner and dance afterward
Photo by Al Levie

As time went on, students at Horlick became engaged in organizing Black History celebrations that helped shape their perspectives, moving them from a "can't do" attitude to a "can do" attitude.

They were finding their voice and agency within the school.

My students began organizing glorious King Day celebrations at Horlick that drew parents and community members into the school. Premier performers and leaders in the community spoke. We garnered support from African American staff, including our Directing Principal. The events were undeniable successes. They were well put together political programs that included a strong Master of Ceremonies, keynote speakers, class act performances from students as well as community artists. Year after year, the highlight of the program was the African American dance group. My daughter Miriam, a talented African dance performer, brought equally talented dancers and musicians to perform for the students. Teachers volunteered to assist in their areas of expertise. The local chapter of the N.A.A.C.P., working with parents and students, provided food and decorations for the soul food dinner.

Kevin Brown on the SAX
Photo by Al Levie

Kevin Brown, a fellow Social Studies teacher at Horlick and talented musician, provided the music at one of our events. Three to four hundred students, parents and community members regularly attended the school events. These student-driven Black History celebrations took two to three months of planning, including establishing goals, identifying allies, and attending to all the details necessary to hold a successful event.

Through this work, African American students were finding hope; they were finding their voice.

Due to the continued success of these events, students built strong agency, positive attitudes and strong relationships in the community.

The MC of one of the King Day events and future S.U.I.T.S leader, LaQuita Barker, recalled the success when she said to me, "*... that kind of put me on a path to advocacy, and stepping into being a leader, you know, not sitting back and being quiet about anything anymore.*"

The stature of Black students rose not only within the school, but with their parents and in the community. Working alongside these students, community members began to see them as a positive force for driving change. The Racine Branch of the N.A.A.C.P. saw the value in their organizing work and heavily invested in them. The students felt nurtured and appreciated by this venerable organization. It led to a long-standing connection between Horlick student activists and the N.A.A.C.P.

Our directing principal at the time, Nola Ratliff, while very supportive of building student success, was simultaneously very nervous about sponsoring the program. She seemed to fear failure. To her, it would have been both demoralizing for the students as well as a poor reflection on the school if the event did not come together. To her credit, however, she lent her full support to the program. The students' success became her success, and in some ways elevated her status within the school district and within the community. She became extremely supportive of the Black students' organizing in the school, and in turn, they supported her.

Students United In The Struggle (S.U.I.T.S)

The classroom work and school-based activities, such as the Black History programs the students developed and participated in, along with their school sponsored trips all contributed to the confidence needed to build an organization that would promote student interests in both the school and in the community.

At Horlick it had become time to push forward on this student-driven initiative to build power among the African American kids.

For every action, there is a reaction.

It was clear to me that if they were going to create real change for themselves, they needed to be part of a larger group that would support them. Brandon, Laqueta, and Kamala's request for support was perfectly timed.

Dick Gregory at NAACP dinner with SUITS leaders
Photo by Al Levie

As with the Latino student organizing, I sought out a community-based organization that the Black kids could partner with that shared their concerns and supported them in their organizing. To me, the N.A.A.C.P. seemed a perfect fit. I solicited around 25 of the Black students to join the N.A.A.C.P. youth arm. My plan was to be the N.A.A.C.P. student advisor at Horlick. I approached Clair, the chair of the N.A.A.C.P. Racine Youth arm, and told her I had 25 youth members. I asked her if I could start a youth chapter at my school. She said that unfortunately, no, they were a city-wide organization and didn't endorse school chapters. Despite my appeal to the state and regional leadership, it was determined that we could not have an N.A.A.C.P chapter at Horlick.

I showed Laquita, one of my African American student leaders, the letter I had received from N.A.A.C.P. Regional staff that determined that we could not have a chapter. After she read the letter, I said, *"Now what?"* LaQuita replied, *"He signed the letter*

'United In The Struggle'." After reading the letter, LaQuesta said, *"Mr. Levie, we will have our own group at Horlick and we will name it, "**Students United In The Struggle**."*

When asked years later what effect the incident had on her and how she came up with the name S.U.I.T.S, LaQuita said it was born of anger. She said, *"They were not in the struggle, we were. I really thought it was going to go through."* She went on to say, *"The leader woke up in me at that point. Thank you, Mr. Levie. Up to that point, I was kind of shy."*

LaQuita continued, *"If you had brought us students with you to that meeting, we would have made them understand who you really were and that we trusted you and so should they."*

After school in my classroom, the students who wanted to form the club met. We read the letter and decided that together, we would become S.U.I.T.S.

Although the attempt to link the group to the NAACP was unsuccessful, it had established a strong relationship with its local leaders, particularly Beverly Hicks, the chapter president at the time. She continued to support all of the students' initiatives, as she had always done. As the students carried on their work in S.U.I.T.S, they maintained a healthy relationship with the N.A.A.C.P, who provided support and guidance in their endeavors.

Following the unsuccessful link to the N.A.A.C.P, I requested that Voces de la Frontera accept them as part of their youth social justice efforts, just as they had done with S.U.F.R.I.R, and they did.

S.U.I.T.S in Washington D.C. 2006

"It was life changing on several levels. It was the first time I ever traveled away from home without my mother or grandmother. We did so many things. We met with Hillary Sheldon of the NAACP, lobbied our legislators, and saw unbelievable historical sights. The trip gave me an opportunity to grow as a person, but also to begin to understand the world in a political way. The highlight of the experience was meeting and spending an afternoon with John Lewis. It was amazing. He was a living legend. Several years later after he passed, I placed a note at the foot of his mural in Atlanta. The note read, "Rest in Power." My time with him was very special."

ADWOA ASENTU (BRITNEY BROWN)

As in the case of the Latino students when they were beginning their organizing efforts, Voces de La Frontera covered the costs for an all-expense paid trip for seven African American students to travel to Washington DC as a part of an effort to build Black youth leadership and nurture black/brown unity in the struggle against oppression.

A diverse group of students was chosen. Among them were athletes, performers, strong students and some that had no interest in school but had a sense of social justice.

S.U.I.T.S students getting a legislative briefing by Hillary Sheldon, Director of the N.A.A.C.P. Washington Bureau
Photo by N.A.A.C.P. Staff

In Washington DC the students were given a glimpse into a larger world. There were several activities planned that helped them grow both as people and as emerging leaders.

At the Center for Community Change, a national organization that builds power among low-income people, especially people of color in order to help them fight for a society where everyone can thrive, organizer Dashaw Hocket led Horlick students in a three-hour workshop. Hillary Sheldon, the N.A.A.C.P. Legislative Liaison, gave them a history lesson of civil rights struggles in the United States. He educated them on current civil rights issues and pending legislation. He provided them with N.A.A.C.P. generated legislative scorecards, which showed the students how their representatives in both the Senate and House voted. The students then spent time lobbying their elected representatives.

Perhaps most meaningful for them was the time they were able to spend with Representative John Lewis.

For many, meeting with John Lewis was life changing. Ambrosia Golden, one of my students, said of the experience, "*... John Lewis met with us for an hour in his office, asking and answering questions. He then took us on a personal tour of the Capitol building and led us onto the floor of the House where he showed us how bills were developed and passed. We received a real political education from this towering figure.*"

Dashaw Hockett, organizer Center for Community Change, leading student leaders in a workshop on community organizing.
Photo Al Levie

The emerging student leaders on this trip were all freshmen. Through their past participation in S.U.I.T.S, all displayed tremendous leadership qualities. It was clear that they understood the importance of this experience, that they knew they would use what they had gained from their time in Washington to help organize their fellow students back home.

The students returned to Horlick ready to do some real work.

Student rally on Monument Square in downtown Racine as part of King Day event
Photo by Al Levie

> *"King Day wasn't just given to us. It took 3 years of getting petitions signed, picketing, lobbying the school board, and joining forces with Voces and NAACP to win this holiday."*
>
> BRITNEY CALLAWAY, SUITS MEMBER

King Day Holiday

The newly trained S.U.I.T.S leaders returned home and began organizing efforts. This included working to get Racine Unified to offer Dr. King's birthday as a school holiday. RUSD, unlike the larger Milwaukee School District or Chicago Public Schools, did not recognize the national holiday.

For three years, S.U.I.T. S worked to secure King Day as a school holiday. They garnered the support of S.U.F.R.I.R, Voces, the local N.A.A.C.P branch, as well as some RUSD Central Office staff and teacher union members. During that time, they strategically picketed at school board meetings. They eloquently spoke before the board and enlisted others in the school and in the community to lend their support. The final push involved lobbying teacher's union negotiators and administrators who were part of the school calendar negotiations. They succeeded in securing the support of both an administrator and a union negotiator, both of whom championed the holiday alongside the students.

After three hard-fought years, they won!

RUSD modified the school calendar, and the Dr. Martin Luther King holiday became a reality.

The author (Al Levie Promoting the King Day event at Horlick)

Immediately following their victory, the school district announced the holiday. The Racine Journal Times ran an editorial sermonizing the students. Paternalistic in tone, the gist of their piece conveyed the hope that now that the students had the day off, they would not just use it to sleep in.

S.U.I.T.S. members didn't let any moss grow under their feet. They immediately began organizing for a meaningful and successful King Day. After the victory, they held a summer rally at the King Center followed by a march to the King statue. They invited the Racine Unified Superintendent and the Mayor to attend, and both did. They asked them if they would participate in a joint event with S.U.I.T.S. on King Day and they both agreed.

This set the stage for a tremendous King Day event.

The students and I organized for two months in an effort to guarantee the day's success. We built a powerful coalition to carry it out. At the center of it was the N.A.A.C.P, Voces de la Frontera, the Racine Unified School District, the City of Racine, and the teacher's union, the Racine Education Association. This coalition, leveraging their relationships, helped raise over $14,000 from local funders. They helped with both the logistics and the development of the program. The event was held at Memorial Hall, a large, city-owned facility in downtown Racine. The mayor helped ensure that the cost was reasonable.

But make no mistake - at the helm were the students.

They were on the planning committee with the N.A.A.C.P. They facilitated and participated in countless meetings, volunteered to do all of the set-up, as well as scripted, MCed and participated in the program. The effort was massive.

We decided that the King Day event hinged on three major components: *Community Service, Social Justice Training, and Celebration,* three tenants of King's life and legacy.

1. At 8:00 AM on the day of the event, the Racine Unified School District provided breakfast for the students, who gathered at Memorial Hall. Following breakfast, students, along with their chaperones, went to various community sites around the city and participated in volunteer work. Students were able to choose their volunteer assignments, and there were several options- anything from spending time with the elderly at a nursing home to cleaning or painting at community centers.

2. The afternoon segment of the program consisted of both a lunch and social justice workshops, hosted by Voces de la Frontera and legal aid. These workshops were extremely relevant. They included educational sessions, including a "Know Your Rights" workshop, where students were informed of their rights as it related to interactions with the police in their schools. Additionally, there was a creative workshop, where students worked together to craft art builds that could be used for future demonstrations, rallies and marches.
3. In the evening, there was a triumphant King celebration that included the full participation of the Racine Branch of the N.A.A.C.P. They provided the soul food meal and volunteered to serve the food to the hundreds of parents, students and community members who attended. The program event was scripted and MCed by the Horlick students. The entertainment was mostly student-driven as well. A topical and relevant keynote speech was issued by Reg Weaver, President of the National Education Association (N.E.A).

Every seat was filled with parents, students, family, friends and community members; there were over 600 people in attendance. In fact, there were so many people who came to attend the event that we filled overflow seating on the balcony in Memorial Hall which held about 150 people. This huge turnout can be attributed to two factors: one, the event, in its entirety, from the food to the entertainment, was free for those in attendance, and two, the students and I put forth tremendous effort to publicize the celebration. For weeks leading up to the King Day program we made telephone calls inviting every African American family at Horlick High School. We asked them how many people would attend from their family and let them know that their participation was on a "first-come-first-serve basis." If they had large families, we told them to come early.

The African American students at Horlick had made their mark. Their pride following the success of this event was unmistakable.

They repeated this activity on a yearly basis.

After the first few years of successful King Day celebrations, Mark Belling, a conservative radio host, blasted the Racine County United Way for contributing to the celebration. He remarked that Voces de La Frontera, one of the program's main sponsors, was a radical, pro-immigrant organization. As a result, United Way dropped its financial contribution for future King Day events. The students, the N.A.A.C.P, Voces de La Frontera, and the Racine Educational Association leadership moved into action, never wavering in their support of the kids or the event. The students managed to secure a meeting with the President of the Racine County United Way. They explained that while Voces did advocate for the rights of immigrants, it was not a radical organization. They went on to further explain that Voces had a tax status as a 501 C3; this tax status can only be attained by non-political organizations. They clarified that Voces held the same status as every other organization to which United Way contributes. The President of United Way reported the details of our meeting to the United Way Board. Ultimately, despite the students' eloquent arguments, the decision was made to pull contributions to the King Day program. It was clear to the students that both Belling and the pro-business United Way Board objected to the afternoon workshops, which served to equip students with the necessary tools not only to keep themselves safe, but to spark change in the communities in which they lived.

United Way's decision not to fund future King Day activities accomplished two things: one, it united a coalition of powerful groups to stand in solidarity with the students, and two, it taught the students a valuable lesson. They learned that no matter how just or righteous the cause, nor how articulate you make your case, those who have power, in the end, decide the outcome.

In this instance, it was business leaders, following a reactionary radio host's demand to defund a student-lead and student-centered day of activity honoring Dr. King, who had the power.

Left to Right: S.U.I.T.S leader Kamala Richardson,
Principal Radcliff, Careen Owens
Photo by Racine Journal Times

Rosa Parks Memorial

The organization that was built as a result of all of S.U.I.T.S' successful activities such as their King Day celebrations allowed the students at Horlick to continue planning and executing powerful events over the years. One of which was a gathering of over 250 people in front of the high school honoring the legacy of Rosa Parks.

S.U.I.T.S leader Kamala Richardson, alongside Racine Civil Rights Icon Coreen Owens and the N.A.A.C.P. Racine Branch President Beverly Hicks gave powerful speeches that day, highlighting Rosa Parks.

They encouraged the students to continue to organize for justice in their schools and in society at large.

And so, they did.

Students demand and win school referendum 2005
Save Our Schools rally
Photo by Allen Levie

Save Our Sports, Save Our Enrichment Programs

In 2005, when a 9.5-million-dollar referendum failed in Racine for school funding, the Superintendent, as quoted in the local newspaper, said, "*... The district would need to close schools and cut all athletics and activities to balance the budget.*" This notion sparked outcry and a movement within the district to petition for a new referendum. Students, teachers and community members were outraged. Students from all socio-economic backgrounds became involved in fighting back against the cuts. The high school activities director organized in an effort to reverse the course. He worked with students on the weekend to collect the required signatures that would force a new referendum. Student activist Xavier Marquez became involved as did many other student activists. They ultimately collected the necessary signatures and delivered them to the School Board.

Students and teachers packed the School Board meeting where a new referendum would be considered. They held a powerful march and rally outside the RUSD Administrative Office prior to the meeting. Over 1,500 students were present. Those that could fit packed into the School Board meeting. Those that couldn't, continued to march and rally outside. Ultimately, as a result of their efforts, the Board was forced to hold a new referendum.

S.U.F.R.I.R. kicked into high gear.

In support of the referendum, they organized a Get Out The vote effort in which over 150 students and teacher chaperones participated. Together, they knocked on thousands of doors, passing out pro-referendum literature. They talked with as many residents as possible, sharing their experiences and perspectives as young people benefiting from these programs in the district. They wore bright yellow t-shirts that read, *"Vote **YES** for us"*. As a result, voters overwhelmingly passed the new referendum. At the School Board, a motion passed in a 5-4 vote to protect school initiatives, not only increased school funding by 10 million dollars, but also prevented cuts to athletics and other activities.

The passage of this resolution can be largely attributed to student activism and leadership.

While the initiative was started by an administrator, it was seen through by seasoned student leaders who had previously led and participated in both G.O.T.V. and immigrants' rights efforts.

Their work brought about the desired results. Together, S.U.I.T.S. and S.U.F.R.I.R. had successfully planned and executed a winning G.O.T.V. strategy.

Clearly, the growing power of both S.U.I.T.S. and S.U.F.R.I.R was being felt at Horlick and throughout the district.

Kamala, a S.U.I.T.S leader at the time of the referendum efforts, later recalled a spontaneous walkout that she led with Xavier's assistance. Kamala said, "... *We marched to [the] Central Office, protesting any cuts to programs at Horlick. Our power was growing.*"

The successful passage of the referendum was a direct result of seasoned student leadership and activism. These students strategically organized a powerful campaign and led door to door canvassing efforts. They involved both teachers and community allies and mobilized hundreds of students to participate with them.

They were rightfully seen as the driving force for preserving their sports and enrichment programs.

CHAPTER 5

EMERGING STUDENT/ TEACHER UNITY

Chilpancingo

Ejido Chillpancino is home to over 60,000 Maquiladora workers
It is located at the foot of Mesa Otay where both the Hyundai
and Metales plants are located. It is extremely polluted
by factories that release toxic waste into the creek
Photo by Al Levie

As the staff sat in the auditorium that day in 2005, contemplating our presentation and their students' courageous testimonials of their journeys over the border to the United States, Kerry, a colleague of mine, turned to me, her eyes filled with tears and her voice shaking with anger. She said to me, "... *Why did you show us this!?*"

It could no longer go unseen or be ignored - teachers at Horlick were beginning to take notice of student organizing. A few were even beginning to see the connection between supporting that organizing and building relationships with the students involved.

That year I, along with my colleague Ryan Knudson, had an opportunity to participate in the *Reality Tour of the Border,* sponsored by Rethinking Schools and Global Exchange. The program was meant to help accelerate teacher understanding of their immigrant students' realities.

The trip was designed to educate teachers on the North Atlantic Free Trade Agreement (N.A.F.T.A.) and Operation Gatekeeper - an immigration and enforcement policy of border patrol that was put in place within six months of the passage of N.A.F.T.A. in 1994. These policies allocated massive resources for beefing up border security in San Diego. In effect, as a result, border crossing was pushed further north across the treacherous desert and mountains.

The goal of the trip was to teach us about the experiences and realities facing the immigrant children we taught every day. Our only obligation after returning back to our school post participating in the program was to share what we had learned with students and with staff.

Bob Peterson, one of the founders of Rethinking Schools and the President of the Milwaukee Teachers Union, sponsored a teacher's writing workshop following the trip. He invited both Ryan and I to participate and asked us to write an article for Rethinking Schools. The resultant piece was published, and it highlighted the immigrant organizing experience at Horlick.

Our visit to both sides of the border was eye-opening. We learned about the sleepy town of Tijuana. Pre-N.A.F.T.A, it was a town with a population of no more than 100,000. In the wake of N.A.F.T.A, it is now over-populated at well over a million.

We visited a makeshift community of 60,000 Maquiladora workers and bore witness to the deplorable conditions in which they lived. Maquiladora is a factory in Mexico run by a foreign company which exports its products back to itself.

Our visit to a modern transmission factory that paid $1.00 per hour for skilled workers was bone-chilling. The work they did was at the same skill level as work I had done 15 years earlier as a machinist. However, there were glaring disparities between the terms of their employment and mine. They worked 10-hour days, experienced poor safety conditions and received a weekly bag of groceries in exchange for their labor. I was paid $18.00 per hour, received paid vacations, health insurance and a promise of a pension. They had a union, however, it was organized by the company, resulting in the representation of the company's interests over those of the workers, whereas I was represented by the International Association of Machinist and Aerospace Workers (I.A.M.A.W.), a powerful, international worker-led union which represented my interests.

The workers and their families lived in squalor and had to truck in their water supply. Theirs was a bleak existence, something I have never had to experience. As a machinist I rented a nice three-bedroom apartment in a two-family flat just blocks from Rock Lake, a summer tourist destination.

On the final day of our stay, we visited the Border Patrol offices, and we were given a presentation highlighting the successes of Operation Gatekeeper. The agent made a power point presentation that proudly painted a picture of how they were able to push undocumented immigrants away, keeping them from crossing the border in San Diego. It showed their ongoing efforts to secure the U.S. border all the way from the Pacific Ocean to the Gulf of Mexico. What he didn't dwell on was the thousands of deaths that had resulted in the perilous journeys across the desert and mountains, the journeys made by some of my students and their families.

What Ryan and I saw left an indelible mark on our souls. We came back ready to educate. We put together a presentation for the teachers at Horlick and were given an opportunity to share what we had seen and what we had learned. Our presentation included a slide show about our trip. I supplied the photos and Ryan presented to the staff.

Two undocumented students, Maria Vital and Jon Salazar joined us on stage and shared their harrowing experiences of crossing over the border with the teachers. Maria had crossed the river and Jon had crossed the desert. Jon, with whom I recently spoke, recalled the experience and said, "*...I was eleven years old when I made the journey. It took me, my mother and my cousin three months to cross. It's something that is painful to recall. We were chased by the Cartel (Mexican Crime Syndicate). We knew if we were caught, they would steal our money and kidnap us for ransom. We were hot during the day, cold at night, and always hungry and thirsty. I feared for my life.*"

Hearing their students share their experiences of crossing the border deeply affected my fellow teachers. Kerry's emotions, her anger, her tears, they were real. But her question, "*...Why did you show us this?*", was rhetorical.

The mission was accomplished. Many of the teachers experienced profound empathy for their students.

They were open to supporting immigrant students in their struggles.

Our relationship with Rethinking Schools connected us with other social justice educators who were doing great work connecting students to issues that affected them. It provided an intellectual framework and a level of legitimacy for the ideas we were promoting among our fellow teachers.

Aaron Eick, Horlick GOTV teacher chaperone
Photo by Al Levie

GOTV 2008

The 2008 Get Out the Vote campaign was a significant leap forward with regard to Horlick staff interaction with student activists. Up to that point, most of the organizing work had been done by me and the students. However, following the educational piece I provided with my colleague about our time spent on the border as well as the many successful events planned by students at Horlick, there was a growing number of teachers who began to see the students as a driving force for positive change in the city and within the school district.

Together they were beginning to build power.

In 2008, for the Get Out The Vote campaign, approximately a dozen Horlick teachers took personal days and joined nearly

350 Horlick students and community volunteers in a door-to-door election day canvassing effort. These teachers used their personal days to volunteer to be drivers and chaperones for the students. They did so because they found value in this powerful service-learning activity. Furthermore, they saw it as an opportunity to build relationships with the students. Aaron Eick, a Horlick Social Studies teacher, recently told me, "*... Yeah, initially I was drawn to it because I thought it was a great teaching activity. Well, originally it was a service-learning teaching activity. But I began to see it as much more as my interaction with the students deepened. I came to understand that it was about building power for both teachers and students, and that my interests were intertwined with the interests of the students.*"

Evolving Dynamic in Teacher/Student Relationship

Jessika White, an African American student, who by her account had a lot to say but kept her opinions to herself, describes herself as shy, except around her friends. Her involvement with S.U.I.T.S. led to her becoming an outspoken advocate for social justice. She planned, executed and became an eloquent spokesperson for the issues and campaigns the group worked on.

In an interview with Jessika, she stated, "*... Teachers began to look at me and other students involved in SUITS in a different way. One particular history teacher began to give us more challenging and relevant work to do.*"

The teachers' expectations had grown, as had Jessika's realization that the oppressed students were capable of much more than she had initially had realized.

At this time, teacher involvement in the struggle grew.

One of the newer, more liberal and union-minded teachers, Aaron Eick, seemed to believe that the students were not serious about making change. Essentially, he seemed to believe they participated in events such as GOTV to get a day off school or time out of class.

However, over time, his active engagement with the students brought him to the realization that student leaders were courageous in standing up to power. In working with the students, he saw how hard they worked, and how much time they invested in themselves and in their school. Jessika said of Aaron, "... *It inspired him to stand up with them [the students] because they believed in what they were doing and it pushed this young union activist teacher to see potential and get involved in student organizing.*"

Aaron corroborated Jessika's perspective. He said, "*I didn't recall ever telling the students that they weren't serious. I joked with them a lot, but didn't really see them as building power.*" He added, "...*over time it changed. The more I was involved with student organizing, the more I realized that they were indeed very serious and very determined.*"

His perspective on the GOTV efforts evolved as well. Aaron stated, "... *I first saw it as a service-learning project. An activity where students could get real life experience on what they were studying. I began to see, however, that the students understood that they were in fact changing the power dynamic in the city. The 10-million-dollar school funding referendum that they won was because of students organizing.*"

Student organizing clearly had an effect on both teachers and students. White teachers began to overcome the stereotype they had developed regarding low achieving students of color as disinterested or passive learners. Their observation of student activism helped them understand that there was more to their students than what met the eye; they began seeing some true potential.

In addition to school staff ramping up their involvement with student organizing, community leaders and organizations also began to see organized students as a powerful force for change.

N.A.A.C.P. Racine Branch President, Beverly Hicks, addressing Horlick students on the importance of registering and voting. This event took place in the parking lot of Horlick High School. It served to energize and organize the hundreds of students that participated in the regular Get Out the Vote door-to-door Day of Action. That year the Horlick students led the largest student Get Out the Vote effort in the country. Photo by Al Levie

Maria Morales, long time Racine community activist, speaking to Horlick students.
Photo by Al Levie

Both Beverly Hicks and Maria Morales are living civil rights icons in Racine. Beverly's participation at Horlick helped us successfully lead African-American history programs and win King Day as an official school holiday in the district. Maria has a long history of working on behalf of immigrants in the city. She has worked both individually with families on immigration and discrimination and harassment issues. Additionally, she worked to organize the community to fight back against the assault from Immigration and Customs Enforcement (I.C.E.) to pass fair and humane immigration reform.

Both Beverly and Maria breathed life into the students' struggles and connected them to the community. Both helped broker my relationship to their respective communities. Both are well-recognized, having led many struggles for human and civil rights. Parents knew that if Maria and Beverly were involved, their kids would be safe and that their work would be meaningful.

Annual Retreat strategic planning session
Photo by Al Levie

Annual Student Retreats

"Mr. Levie, we would like to give you some money for the organizing you do." I was honored that Sister Virginia of the Dominican Sisters offered us a contribution for our work. The Dominican Sisters have been an institution in Racine for progressive politics. They participated in all of the marches, rallies, and press conferences sponsored by Voces. Their representatives often spoke and gave a religious perspective on why progressive immigration reform was necessary. I recall that Sister Virginia made the offer to financially support our organizing on the bus ride back to Racine from a march in Madison that the students had organized in support of in-state tuition for undocumented students.

I asked Sister Virginia, *"How much money do they have to give?"*

She asked me, *"How much do you need?"* I picked a number out of the air, and said, *"$20,000."*

She said, "... *Well that's a lot of money. What will you use it for?"* to which I replied, *"Leadership development,"* She asked me for a proposal of our work, which I prepared and gave to the Sisters. In return, we received $14,000 in funding. During the first few years of our organizing efforts, we used the funding to sponsor leadership trips to Washington D.C. However, as time passed and our student organizations began to grow, we had so many emerging leaders that we then decided we should use the money for local training and planning retreats.

The local, three-day summer retreats included organizing training and movement building activities such as street theater, poster making, as well as slogan and chant writing. Additionally, the students participated in fun team-building field trips.

Over the years, hundreds of students have participated in these retreats.

> *"Retreats offered us an opportunity for our voices to be heard. Our opinions were respected. We grew as people and left empowered."*
>
> MARIA VITAL,15-YEAR-OLD STUDENT LEADER.

CHAPTER 6

HORLICK TEACHERS BEGIN BUILDING GRASSROOTS POWER

"We will expose the district plan for what it is, a scheme to save money by increasing class size, laying off staff, and killing our successful drama, music, and art programs."

DON YOUNG, HORLICK MUSIC TEACHER

In 2005, there was a surge in teacher activism as the district prepared to move to block scheduling, a shift from 50-minute to 90-minute class periods.

Historically, teachers' unions had been established to represent the interests of teachers and students and to advocate for sound educational policy. Many local teachers' unions operated within a strict hierarchy which was reinforced by state and national affiliates. In top-down fashion, the leaders of these locals often act on behalf of the members rather than democratically organizing those rank-and-file members to lead. The staff and elected leaders handle grievances, negotiate wages, and sit on various joint educational committees for the members. Members pay dues for services offered by paid staff and leadership. This was essentially the state of the Racine Educational Association (R.E.A.) when I started teaching at Horlick in 2000.

At Horlick, however, we began organizing members to effect policies both in RUSD and within the R.E.A.

In 2005, the proposed switch to block scheduling was an issue that led to bottom-up teacher organizing at Horlick.

Across the district, many high school teachers believed that block scheduling would devastate our district. They saw it as a scheme to eliminate jobs and lower the educational standards state-wide, and they believed that it needed to be stopped. These were the sentiments of the vast majority of high school teachers across the district.

As a Horlick High union representative, I heard my members loud and clear.

At a Back-to-School picnic, Horlick's principal announced that block scheduling would begin during the next school year, and that we would spend the present year getting ready for the transition. I raised my hand and told the teachers not to count on it; that it wasn't a foregone conclusion.

A week later, the Racine Education Association Executive Director at the time, Dennis Wiser, told a room full of high school teachers that it was going to happen. *"...No sense grumbling about it. We couldn't stop it",* he said.

The Racine Unified School District and the R.E.A seemed to be on the same page.

As a teacher with extensive community and labor organizing experience, Wiser's words didn't sit well with me. At our regularly-held building meeting at Horlick we decided to put forward a proposal at the next R.E.A. Representative Assembly that would oppose block scheduling. The Representative Assembly was the body of elected union representatives from all the school buildings in the district; its function was to set policy.

At the Assembly, on behalf of Horlick members, I put forward a motion that the R.E.A oppose block scheduling. A lively debate ensued about both the merits of block scheduling and possible motives for why the district would want to switch to a block schedule. Many saw it as an attempt to lay off staff and believed that the 90-minute schedule would ultimately have negative effects on student learning, teaching conditions and overall morale.

The motion passed.

A committee was subsequently formed to launch a campaign to oppose block scheduling.

At the time, Dean Petit, a member of the union Executive Committee and a veteran of the teachers' strikes of the 1970's was appointed by the union President to chair the block scheduling committee. He approached me after the Rep Assembly and said that he had no experience with the type of motion I had presented and the body had passed or the kind of work that would follow.

He asked me to help, and I agreed.

In preparation for the first block scheduling meeting, I created a simple agenda and shared it with Dean who facilitated the meeting. Approximately forty high school teachers were in attendance at this meeting, and there was broad representation from all the high schools.

Our agenda was approved by those present. We first discussed and brainstormed the possible pros and cons of block scheduling and listed them on the board. Together, we developed a coherent message about why block scheduling was the wrong approach for the district at that time. We then developed a targeted list of the groups we needed to reach with our message in order to help us stop block scheduling. In small groups we focused on specific messages and worked to identify individuals we needed to approach for support. As a large group we decided on our next step - to invite the district representatives leading the block scheduling initiative to a meeting at the R.E.A. office. They accepted. Almost fifty union-member high school teachers met with the district representative.

Over time it became increasingly clear to the members that the block scheduling plan was flawed. They continued to express their disapproval.

One Horlick teacher conveyed the thinking of many in the room when he said, "*... We will expose the district plan for what it is, a scheme to save money by increasing class size, laying off staff and killing our successful drama, music, and art programs.*"

I was perceived by the district as a leader in the movement to stop block scheduling. As a result, they invited me to visit a school district which served as a model for what they wanted to develop in Racine via block scheduling. It was an attempt to convince me that this shift was the right choice. I agreed to go, but I stipulated that I needed to bring two fellow teachers with me. They agreed, so off we went to the suburban showcase school.

Although newer, the building had a similar physical capacity as the four main Racine high schools. We immediately learned, however, that its enrollment was half ours. We had around 2,400 students in a building that had a capacity of 1,200. This school, with a capacity of 1,400 students, had around 1,200 students.

The passing time experience between classes was also vastly different from what we experienced on an hourly basis at Horlick. Students walked at a comfortable pace, chatting with fellow students. At Horlick it was shoulder-to-shoulder. Students wanting to get to class on time had to be focused and quick enough to break through the walls of students that clogged the halls.

We interviewed teachers from various departments and got mixed responses regarding block versus traditional scheduling. Some of the Industrial Education and Science teachers were enthusiastic, while the Math, English, and Social Studies teachers were not. The latter raised issues regarding student focus, highlighting the difficulty of remaining on task for 90 minutes. During our class observations, we noticed that on average, there were 45 minutes of instruction and the other 45 minutes were generally allocated for student-directed studying of new material or completion of worksheets.

The real eye opener came when we talked to one of the department chairs who informed us that test scores had fallen with the new block schedule, and that next year they were going to return to the former schedule.

The administrator who brought us in to observe met me in the cafeteria and asked for our thoughts. I explained to him that we would bring our findings to the high school Representative Assembly, but that initially we were not impressed. I shared with him that we were told that they were reverting back to the regular schedule the following year. He became visibly upset. He told me that there were powerful interests in the district that wanted this to go through. Were that not the case, he told us, there would be significant cuts to educational programs. I told him that the decision was not mine; rather, the union would decide. I also told him that we would fight any and all attempts to water down or cut resources for education in Racine.

Rank and file teacher power at Horlick was growing.

We decided to create a block scheduling informational sheet and distribute it to the parents at Parent Teacher Conferences. We solicited S.U.I.T.S. and S.U.F.R.I.R. to oppose block scheduling. They agreed, and decided that they would pass out the fact sheets at the entrances to the school on parent teacher conference days.

This action was significant. It showed that teachers and students were finding common ground and acting together based upon their mutual interests.

The movement opposing block scheduling now included teachers, students and parents. The district withdrew their block scheduling proposal.

We had stopped block scheduling in its tracks.

As important as stopping the hastily thrown together block schedule was, it was equally, if not more important for teachers in the building to understand that if they were united with one another and with their students, they could directly impact district policy.

> *"When he came into the room, he changed it from a class to a fearful situation. They are out of control, so you don't know what to expect. When I got home and told my grandmother she said she was very pleased and happy to know we had a teacher that would protect us kids."*
>
> Tara Harris, African American History student.

Standing Up To The Police

An incident occurred while I was union president at Horlick that challenged me to strongly advocate for my students, despite mixed feelings in the building among staff regarding my actions as it relates to the police.

I knew it would be controversial because a foundation of building power is unity.

Ultimately, however, justice trumps unity every time.

"Mr. Levie, the police are at the door." Somewhere in the back of my mind, I was hearing someone pulling at my classroom door. During most of my classes, particularly this African American History class, the first 5 minutes are spent standing in front of the students and hooking them into learning. Usually, that meant making a dramatic statement about their lives or recalling something happening at the school and finding a way to relate it back to what we were learning in the class.

I learned early on that without totally connecting with my students right off the bat, I would miss the opportunity to have them engage in learning in a meaningful way.

Although it threw me off my game, I went to the door and unlocked it, asking the policeman if I could help him. He pushed the door wide open, came through it, and said an emphatic, *"No!"* He then pointed his finger at a student sitting at the back of the room and signaled to him to come with him. Another student sitting close to where the policeman stood raised up the desk he was sitting at and banged it loudly on the floor. The policeman jumped, the students all laughed, and then the officer said, *"I'll take all of you in!"*

I saw red. I raised my hand palm out and gestured to my student to hold on, to stay where he was. He stopped.

I then turned to the policeman and asked, *"Do you have a warrant?"*

It was then that all hell broke loose. He and another policeman, who was lurking in the hallway, shouted out, *"If you don't move from the door, you will be arrested for obstructing an investigation!"* They screamed it out twice.

I looked at the student, who didn't seem to be very bothered by being called out by police, and decided to let him go along. I suggested he go with them if he liked. He went with them, and within three minutes was back at my door to be let in, no worse for the wear.

Brittany, a student who was in a seat next to the door, could hear the policeman talking with my principal in the hallway.

"Mr. Levie," she said, *"...the police are telling lies about you to the principal."*

I went out into the hallway and listened. Sure enough, the policeman was misconstruing what had happened. I interjected, directing my comments to the principal, and said, *"What is being stated is not true. I did not prevent the policeman from entering the room."*

The policeman said, *"If you don't go into your room, I'll arrest you right now."*

I looked at him in disbelief and anger. He had come into my classroom and disrupted learning for a trivial matter. I was ready to get arrested. I just stood there.

He said it again.

The principal, in a panicky voice said, *"Please, Mr. Levie, go in your room. Please!"*

I looked at her and realized she was scared, and decided that if I disobeyed her, I could be fired for insubordination. I decided to go back to the class.

It took me a few moments to settle the students upon returning to the room. I used it as a teachable moment. I asked them why they thought we had a police presence in the school, why they were patrolling. I asked them to consider the effect of their presence on the school environment. The discussion contributed to a productive lesson. The Jim Crow era, which I was teaching about, became real to the students that day. It helped them process how Jim Crow laws and their enforcement were a necessary part of an oppressive system; those police then (and now) played a critical role in maintaining the status quo or existing order at any expense. Authority was imperative for the maintenance of power. They saw the parallels.

The next day, I was called down to the principal's office. The policeman who had come to my room the day before was there waiting for me with the principal. I was asked to sit down. The officer, on the other hand, stood over me and pulled out a ticket. He handed it to me and said that it was for obstructing an investigation. He told me that he wanted to bring me down to the station yesterday, but his superiors told him not to. The ticket was for $455.50.

He did as the police are known to do. In a patronizing manner, he explained why I was receiving the ticket, and asked me if I understood. I replied, *"Yes."*

I told the students in the classroom that I had received a ticket. They were furious. They said the charge wasn't justified and asked, *"What are you going to do?"*

I said, *"I'm going to fight it and under no circumstances am I going to pay the ticket."*

I asked them if they would be willing to testify as to what happened.

They all wanted to.

I called the Racine Education Association President and explained what happened. He secured a lawyer who often represents union members. A court date was set and I invited eight of my students to go to court with me.

The plan was that four students would be sequestered for possible testimony, and four would sit in on the proceedings.

The proceedings were quite eventful. My lawyer made the case that I shouldn't have been ticketed. I was protecting the children, that the classroom was my domain and that I had a right to ask the officer for a warrant. It was clarified that I did, in fact, let the officer into the room and allow the student to leave with him.

The City Attorney argued that the police had permission to be in the school, and I had no right to stop them from entering the classroom. The police officer testified that, in fact, I would not let him into the room, and was taunting him when he was in the hallway.

My students were upset that the policeman was lying. They started to talk excitedly about it to each other. The judge banged his gavel and told them that if they didn't quiet down, they would be removed from the courtroom.

I was called to testify about what happened. I simply told the truth.

The judge ruled in my favor, and the crowd erupted. As we were leaving the courtroom, both the police and the City Attorney were shouting at the judge, explaining why he had made the wrong decision. The City Attorney went on to appeal the decision to a higher court. That higher court ultimately ruled against me.

The case was then kicked back to the municipal court for sentencing. I told my union that I was not going to pay any fines, and that I would instead opt for going to jail.

On the day of the hearing, I didn't attend. Instead, someone had paid the reduced fine of $200.00 for me.

To this day, I don't know who paid for it.

Following the issuance of the ticket, the Racine Unified School District immediately sent me a notice to come to the main office for a hearing and instructed me to bring union representation. As soon as I got that notice, I alerted the students, parents, community members and some local political figures. They began contacting the district, telling them that there should be no discipline. The district undoubtedly felt the heat. They postponed the hearing twice. After the ruling of the municipal judge in my favor, the district sent me a letter stating that there would be no hearing, that the case was closed. I was infuriated. The students and I were the ones who were wronged. I went to the union and told the staff that I wanted a meeting with the school Superintendent in order to discuss this issue. If he refused, I let him know that I would file a grievance and possibly sue the district.

The Superintendent at the time, Jim Shaw, granted me and my union representative a meeting. The meeting opened with him asking me why I had wanted to meet. I told him I was there to confront him about his weak leadership. I told him that he had an obligation to protect his teachers, and that in my case, he had failed to do so. It shook him to the core. He stated that when there is police involvement, they have the power to override any school authority, including the Principal and the Superintendent. We talked in circles. In an exasperated voice he said, *"Well what do you want?"*

I told him that I wanted to establish a new policy in the schools regarding police presence, one that included police only being able to interact with the students in either the presence of an administrator or a parent. I set forth the notion that if a child needed to be questioned, an administrator, teacher, or hall monitor needed to escort that child to the principal's office. I went on to state that the parent of that child needed to be present in order for the police to question the student. I also asked that a task force be established to examine the question of safety and police presence in the schools. I expressed that I wanted to be a member of the task force.

He agreed.

R.U.S.D implemented my suggestions. They did not, however, allow for my participation on the task force. The Superintendent informed me that I was not allowed to participate due to some individuals' refusal to work alongside me.

Me standing up for my student, as well as for myself and involving the students, their parents, fellow teachers, and my union was important for the culture of Horlick and for the district as a whole. There were valuable lessons learned.

Through this experience, both teachers and students learned that they had power if they chose to exercise it.

The administration and the police were clearly in league together. If I had done nothing following the situation with the police in my classroom, I would have been fired. This was not the case, however.

The teachers, in observing my actions, learned that with student, teacher, and union support, winning is possible. For the students, it drove home the realization that there were teachers that would take risks on their behalf. It cemented my relationship with the African-American and Latino students.

This event created a vibrant dialogue and debate among my fellow teachers about the role of the police in schools. A consensus was beginning to emerge among the staff and students. Some former ardent supporters of police in the schools questioned the ticketing of a fellow teacher, particularly someone they liked and someone who had stood up for them as their union representative. It also sent a signal to teachers that they, too, could stand up with dignity for what was right and not fear for their jobs.

The incident shined a spotlight and put a lot of pressure on the district. They were forced to clarify their stances and make policy changes related to policing in the schools.

Because the incident was public, the local media gave it coverage from the very beginning. There were several articles written and lots of blog activity. It raised community awareness and concerns regarding police presence and conduct in the schools.

Below are but a few bloggers' comments from differing points of view regarding the incident:

Denis Navratil 5/29/2009 5:19 PM

This is the same teacher who organizes kids to lobby in Madison for illegal immigrants' rights. A real advocate for law breakers he is. He should be a public defender, not a teacher.

Casper Hamilton 5/30/2009 11:48 AM

It is clear that the officer should not have written the ticket. The officer should have taken the teacher to the side and explained the current rights and responsibilities of the teacher and himself in that situation.

The officer made a real mistake. The teacher is responsible for the lives of the students in their class and in the building. If they simply handed over students to unfamiliar people every time they came to a classroom we all would be in trouble. I have been inside of a school with police officers. They do not wear police uniforms and I cannot say if the teachers are familiar with every officer in the building. Some of the police look disheveled while working in the schools: jeans, wrinkled clothes, and mismatched shirts.

I am friends with several Unified teachers and I have a child that attends a RUSD school. Most teachers that I have talked to seem to believe there is a need for some police presence. However, an officer who gives a ticket to a teacher who seems to have asked a clarifying question is unjustifiable. He must not understand that the school is NOT the street; and teachers are not deputy police officers.

I am saddened to see that principals in our schools are not creating an environment in which teachers and other adults working in the building can understand each other where all can work to create a positive learning environment for students.

Anonymous 5/29/2009 4:06 PM

This Levie character sounds like a real trouble maker. Head of the union and likes to interfere with police investigations. A fine person to be educating today's youth and I'm sure a Unified All-Star employee!

Cecilia Leal

"For everyone who knows Levie, knows why he asked for a warrant. His students are his children and he is an amazing teacher!! He showed his students to speak their minds. Stand up for what they believe. A Lot of people think it is wrong. And that's just because he is right!! How many people do you think there are in Unified, that care as much as he does??? I thank Mr. Levie, for showing me what power we young people have when we use it the right way!!"

CHAPTER 7

HORLICK STUDENTS CATAPULT TO NATIONAL PROMINENCE

March 2006: Horlick students leading the 30,000 strong marchers in Milwaukee against HR 4437
Photo by Al Levie

"Me and Viviana were holding hands on the front lines. When we got to the bridge, I turned around and told Viviana to turn around and see what we were doing. It was an overwhelming feeling. I was just like; you know we did this. It was like the highest moment of my life. All the meetings, all the late nights. It paid off. There were thousands."

XAVIER MARQUEZ, MARCH 23, 2006.

Horlick Black and Brown Students Lead Immigrant Rights Marches in Milwaukee

On March 23, 2006, immigrants and their allies launched the largest protest in Wisconsin History: over 30,000 strong.

It centered around two issues:

The first was the fight back against Congressmen Sensenbrenner's anti-immigration bill, HR 4437, a bill that passed the U.S. House of Representatives in December of that year, making it a felony to be undocumented in the United States and imposing penalties on employers who hired the undocumented. It also included legislation to erect additional fences along the U.S-Mexican border.

The second was in response to Wisconsin Governor Jim Doyle's AB 69, a bill signed into law on March 10th 2006. It excluded people who were undocumented from receiving driver's licenses.

Although Racine youth only numbered in the hundreds among the thousands of protestors at this march, their voice was important, and they participated in a meaningful way.

Leading up to the march, Horlick students had done a lot of work organizing on the issues. Only months before, at a press conference in Racine, Governor Doyle, when confronted by Horlick S.U.F.R.I.R members, had pledged to veto AB 69. During this press conference, Doyle turned to Viviana Pastrana, a straight-A, Mexican-born student and made a promise to Veto the bill. However, following that press conference, he quickly began waffling on his support of immigrants, and his staff ignored repeated calls for a meeting with Horlick students and Voces leaders. It wasn't until Voces picketed his fundraiser in early February that he acquiesced and agreed to a meeting later that month at his Milwaukee office.

Christine Neuman-Ortiz, Executive Director of Voces de la Frontera, myself, and Viviana Pastrana met with Governor Doyle to try and secure a commitment for his continued support for vetoing the bill. Viviana reminded Governor Doyle of the promise he had made to her. She asked him if he was going to honor his commitment to veto AB 69. Governor Doyle turned three shades of red. He tried to explain why he could no longer honor his promise.

In a recent discussion with Viviana she said, *"...The Governor betrayed and lied to us. I was shocked that he went back on his word and would not listen to reason. He saw no further than beyond his own interests. At that moment I felt defeated but then got mad. We could not let this setback stop us and we needed to continue to fight for our rights."*

Viviana learned an important lesson that day. She came to understand that politics isn't about trust, but rather about power. Her report back to S.U.F.R.I.R served to motivate the group and resulted in Racine organizing a significant turn out for the march in Milwaukee.

Two powerful Horlick youth leaders spoke to thousands of supporters of immigration reform at the rally in Milwaukee in Zeidler Park. Xavier Marquez provided powerful testimony about why the Sensenbrenner bill needed to be defeated and why immediate immigration reform legislation was necessary. I couldn't have been prouder of both Xavier and Viviana that day. I was concerned that Xavier would be too nervous to express exactly how he felt, so I wrote a short speech for him. When I gave it to him, Xavier said, *"Mr. Levie, I need to put things in my own words."*

It was a great moment. Xavier gave such a powerfully moving speech that he was quoted extensively in the Milwaukee media. Viviana gave a rousing speech in Spanish. I didn't understand the words, but we were all inspired by her passion. The crowd erupted in thunderous applause. In interviews for this book, both

Xavier and Viviana stressed again and again the importance of their participation in S.U.F.R.I.R. and the significance of their rise to leadership in their lives. Xavier talked about how he became a mentor for other students who were struggling with their identity, and how they chose a path to be like him rather than involved in dangerous street activity. Viviana told me, *"Mr. Levie, it was a momentous event for both of us."*

Three Horlick S.U.F.R.I.R. students- left to right: Dianir Villarreal, Cecilia Leal, and Bianca Quintero leading the hundreds of students in Milwaukee who struck that day for immigrant rights
Photo by Al Levie

Day Without Latinos: May 1st, 2006

On May 1st, 2006, Voces launched a general strike that resulted in hundreds of businesses shutting down and thousands of workers and students staying away from work and school. Over 60,000 people marched in Milwaukee, both in support of immigrant rights and against the draconian HR 4437, a bill sponsored by Congressman Sensenbrenner from Wisconsin.

This bill criminalized anyone who helped the undocumented stay in this country. There was great fear from family members, teachers and social workers that they could be charged with felonies for not turning in those they associated with who were undocumented.

In Racine, hundreds of students, relatives and community members joined the protest, in which Horlick students played a pivotal role.

HR 4437 made felons of the undocumented and anyone who assisted the undocumented in coming to or staying in the United States.

Horlick student, Maria Vital, addressing the Day Without Latinos crowd of over 60,000 people in Milwaukee on May 1, 2006
Photo by Al Levie

Racine student participation was organized under the leadership of S.U.F.R.I.R and S.U.I.T.S.

S.U.I.T.S. students marching in solidarity with the Immigrant community
Photo by Al Levie

Xavier Marquez, Horlick S.U.F.R.I.R. leader, at
a funder's convention in Denver
Photo by Al Levie

Horlick S.U.F.R.I.R Gains National Attention

The 2006 immigrant rights marches put S.U.F.R.I.R on the map. Funders became interested in the group's activities. Xavier Marquez, S.U.F.R.I.R's president, was invited to present to a funder's two-day conference in Denver, Colorado about student organizing. I accompanied Xavier and assisted him with his presentation. The funders were impressed, and as a result invited us to apply for a student organizing grant. We did so and were given enough money to hire a full-time youth organizer.

In 2007, Voces hired a youth organizer to build chapters in the high schools in both Milwaukee and Racine. It is important to note that the hiring committee included Horlick students. The students knew what they were looking for in terms of support for organizing in their school. With the hiring of Melanie Benesh, the student arm of Voces de la Frontera became a permanent feature of this premier immigrant rights and social justice organization in Wisconsin.

Melanie assisted me at Horlick in helping students develop plans, organize events and provide valuable feedback in their efforts. Her primary responsibility, however, was to build S.U.F.R.I.R school clubs at the other high schools in Racine and in Milwaukee. Within no time, there were chapters at Racine Park and Racine Case High Schools. Within two years, seven high school chapters were organized in Milwaukee.

S.U.F.R.I.R.'s expansion to other schools in Racine and Milwaukee had a positive impact both on student organizing at Horlick as well as on individual students. Horlick students were looked up to and admired as being the first to organize. They shared their experiences and expertise and gave leadership to the other chapters. Students in various chapters met weekly with student leaders from Racine and planned city-wide activity. They came together to work on statewide and national organizing efforts.

The shared experiences and relationships that Horlick students developed with their counterparts from other schools helped them grow and evolve.

CHAPTER 8

A NEW WAVE OF CONSCIOUSNESS EMERGES

Teachers and students demonstrating inside the Wisconsin State Capitol against Governor Walker's Act 10. Horlick Y.E.S. student leaders can be seen top center
Photo by Mike Pope

In 2010, Former Wisconsin Governor Scott Walker's Act 10 struck a match that lit a fire under all public workers.

With the passage of Act 10, Walker had radicalized us. For teachers around the state, its passage crystallized the understanding that we stood to lose many of the significant gains we had fought for and won over the past century.

Overnight, Act 10 changed the balance of power in school districts all across Wisconsin. It stripped teachers of our ability to bargain for wages for anything except cost-of-living increases tied to the rate of inflation in the state. It forced us to re-certify our union rights in the workplace every year. Recertification meant securing a "yes" vote for over 51% of each bargaining unit in order for schools to keep their unions. To complicate matters, not voting registered as a "no" vote.

Emboldened school district administrators understood the power they had been handed, and they moved quickly to make changes in an effort to weaken the power of teachers and our unions.

Melissa Zeien, an extraordinarily gifted French teacher with two years teaching experience at Horlick at the time of Act 10's passage, shared with me in an interview her evolving teacher's union consciousness. During talks with her, she provided insight into her understanding of how important student support for teachers was, as well as how teacher support of students was for the well-being of both.

During her first two years of teaching, like most beginning teachers, she hadn't done anything outside of her classroom. She said, *"I had heard of S.U.F.R.I.R and S.U.I.T.S, but didn't think much about them. I just didn't see the connection; my job was to show up to school, get to know my kids, teach French and then go home."* Most of her students were white, with a smattering of students of color.

She went on to say, *"Act 10 changed everything."*

I asked her what changed. She replied, *"I remember there being a meeting in the library. It was bigger than any union meeting I'd ever been to. More teachers showed up to it than ever, and everybody looked scared, and I didn't really understand why they were scared. Because at that point, I'd only been teaching for two years, so I barely understood pensions. I barely understood health insurance. I barely understood any of it. I just remember looking around at adults who looked a lot older than me, and they looked so scared. I remember going to that meeting, and I remember all of them saying, 'This is important.'"*

Melissa continued on to say, *"... I just started listening to the people around me. I started talking to you. I started talking to*

Aaron. I started talking to Pete. I started talking to your wife, Jen, and I just started getting to know people who knew more than me, having conversations about stuff I'd never talked about before."

In her recollections of that time in her life, she said, "... *[I remember] I got a call at 3 in the morning from a union brother saying, 'If you're feeling sick in the morning, meet us at the Labor Center at 7AM. We're going to Madison.'"*

"I remember I called my friend Kristin and I said, 'I don't know what to do. What are you doing?' And she said, 'I'm gonna do whatever you're doing.' And I was like, 'okay, we're going to Madison.' And that's when it changed. That's when everything changed."

I asked her if she saw the kids participating in the marches. She said, *"I did."*

She continued on, saying, "...*What really struck me was that I saw kids who were in the classes I taught. I think that's what hit me. I saw kids all the time doing stuff in our school, but I didn't really know them, so it didn't really mean much to me. But I remember I saw, I think his name was Shawn, he was one of my first students, a young Black child. I really really loved him. I was really touched that he was there. I was really moved, and I asked him why he had come, and he asked me the same question. He said he wanted to be there, because he felt like he wanted to support the teachers. He knew it was a big deal. He knew we were scared. He knew we were upset, and I said I was there because I knew we were upset, and I knew we were nervous, and I was trying to learn more. I think we were both just really young people learning together."*

"I felt connected to my students at that age because I was so young. They were young, and I think we were both learning about politics and the world together. You know I was so young. Al, I had never learned Social Studies in that way before."

I asked Melissa how she felt about the two busloads of Horlick students, mostly black and brown, who skipped school and came to Madison to support their teachers that day.

Melissa's response was insightful. She said, "*... They were indirectly affected, but they directly cared about me. I don't know if I thought about it much then. But thinking back on it now, I think it's tremendous, because I now know a lot about the livelihoods of those students and their families. I now appreciate what you had said to me back then so much, 'That people who don't have much to give, give the most.' I swear, it changed my life forever.*"

Melissa continued in her testimony to say, "*...I started to appreciate these students. As a person, I recognize in myself the capacity to give until I don't have any more, and I see that same characteristic in those kids. A lot of them come from very little, if not nothing. And they just have this deep well of giving and love. It's really emotional when you think about it...*"

"*...It's so natural for them to give. I hope that answers the question. That's how it made me feel. I was touched that kids who either: A) didn't understand the situation fully, or B) did understand, and still gave a shit, despite all the stuff they were dealing with still showed up for us. That's remarkable!*"

I asked Melissa how her level of involvement with the union and student activists changed as a result of Act 10.

She said, "*My level of involvement went from probably a two to a ten. I was at every meeting. I was on the phone constantly. I was engaged with a group of teachers and students who were starting to get involved in projects and protests and marches. From then on, from 2011 for as long as I worked at RUSD, it never stopped. My foot was on the gas, and it never let up. Never, ever, ever, ever. My involvement with the kids was a ten, and it was always at a ten. I feel like once they got involved in going to Madison with us, I did the same thing for them. I think, in a lot of ways, they had always been involved in really, really amazing project-based learning at school with you and S.U.F.R.I.R and going out into the communities. But I feel like they went from being students to being student-activists really quick, and their involvement with us was at the same level, a 10, at every meeting we showed up to. They were right there at every project we were doing. They were somehow involved in every march we were on...."*

"... I intersected with the kids because I realized that what was happening to me [Act 10] was not just a teacher thing. Whatever the hell happened to us eventually happened to all those kids. It was happening in those buildings. So, once we all wrapped our minds around that idea, it didn't make sense for us to be separate anymore. It didn't make sense for it to be a "teacher" problem, because whatever was going to be a teacher problem from then on in public education was going to affect them as a student problem, and those kids knew it, and the teachers who were zoned-in knew it, too."

In the course of writing this book, I interviewed several teachers who had similar perspectives on how the passage of Act 10 in 2010 changed them. They spoke to me about how it changed their relationships with the students. Many came to believe that students had, as they did, come to a new awareness, finally understanding the need for teacher-student unity.

What they didn't fully understand, however, was that despite their newfound revelations about the need for unity with students, the students had been reaching out and involving teachers in their struggle for justice since 2003.

I can vividly recall this period in my life. I remember feeling a rush of emotions: ashamed, elated, validated and grateful. As a teacher, it was remarkable to watch those very same students, who had been so marginalized, who had struggled for justice for so many years, standing up for us, when we rarely stood up for them. Perhaps their oppression has given them insights about the system that we as teachers were just beginning to understand. They had learned lessons of unity that our collective consciousness as teachers had forgotten over time- lessons that were just beginning to emerge again.

PART 2

2011-2019

CHAPTER 9

YOUTH EMPOWERED IN THE STRUGGLE - Y.E.S.: A POWERFUL FORCE FOR CHANGE

2012 student-led annual May Day March in Milwaukee
Photo by Valeria Ruiz Lia Suarez

Black, White and Brown student unity became a reality with the formation of the new student club at Horlick- Y.E.S.

One plus one = three; Y.E.S. was more than the sum of its parts.

On a drive home from a national *Dream Act* training in Minneapolis, my students, along with Milwaukee S.U.F.R.I.R. students had a discussion about creating one singular student organization. Kennia Coronado, a former S.U.F.R.I.R leader and current PHD candidate, said of this idea, *"It was really just thinking about how most of the issues that we were confronting were just intersectional and overlapped in nature. There were issues around class. There were issues around race and ethnicity. And you know, all the other marginal identities that overlap with many of the people that were in the group. So, I think that was really what led to trying to form some sort of revamped student organization that really embraced [the issues] that all of us were confronting."*

It was then that S.U.F.R.I.R and S.U.I.T.S evolved into one united group named Y.E.S. African Americans who had wanted their own organization in order to strengthen their voice and pursue their interests in the schools and in the community had decided that it was time to unify with all students on social justice. They came up with the name Youth Empowered in The Struggle (Y.E.S.) They shared their name and their idea with students in their respective school clubs and it became official.

Y.E.S. began organizing and politicizing Black, Brown, and White working-class students on their issues. The synergy and unity that was created among these students began to show. White students were beginning to see that they had more in common with their Black and Brown peers than they ever knew. Y.E.S. was now the vehicle for building unity and power among the students at Horlick. It was bolstered and supported by the Racine Education Association and its members, and had a strong base of community support.

Staffing the organization began in 2007 with the hiring of Voces youth organizer Melanie Benesh, who played a strong role in the success of Y.E.S. Staffing afforded students closer attention in the planning and execution of events. With Melanie's assistance, students became better prepared and more deeply organized. She was able to offer leadership development opportunities that, as a full-time classroom teacher, I could not provide. Melanie had previously expanded S.U.F.R.I.R to include four high schools in Racine and seven in Milwaukee. She continued as the youth organizer for three more years before leaving to pursue a law degree at Georgetown University. The formation of Y.E.S. happened shortly before the hiring of a new Y.E.S. organizer, Kate Werning.

Kate, like Melanie, had recently graduated from college. She had a strong sense of social justice and a mind for organizing work. She remained a youth organizer in Y.E.S. for Voces for five years. Both Melanie and Kate's work had a lasting impact on student organizing in Wisconsin.

It was at this time that my role in student organizing shifted from that of teacher-organizer to teacher-club advisor. Prior to funding and the hiring of paid staff, I gave full support to all of the activities and events organized by S.U.F.R.IR. and S.U.I.T.S. The newly hired organizing staff took over the primary responsibility for working with students on a day-to-day basis in order to ensure the success of events, the expansion of student participation, and continued leadership development. They became responsible for the numerous logistical arrangements involved in organizations such as these- and there were many.

The relationship between me and the youth organizers was an important and primary one. As their teacher and the club advisor, the students and their parents trusted me to do what was right for them. In order to further develop the students and to grow student power, the students needed to trust the youth organizers; I facilitated that trust. In order for the work to be successful, the students needed to feel the same level of trust for their organizers that they felt for me. As a Horlick staff member, I had to ensure that student involvement with Y.E.S. was a positive experience. Further, I had to ensure that at no time would students ever be put in harm's way. I took my responsibility very seriously. As such, I stayed actively involved in all aspects of the student's work. I was part of the hiring committee for all the youth organizers. I supervised them and acted as a mentor, speaking with them on the phone almost daily. They took their direction from me in their work with the students. I attended all of the Horlick chapter meetings and worked with the students and the organizers to help craft the agendas. I attended almost all of the major events, participating in some capacity. Although I was not their boss, I sat on the policy board of Voces de la Frontera as its Racine teacher advisor representative for over ten years. When

I retired, my co-advisor Aaron Eick became the Racine teachers board representative for Voces.

I grew to have a great deal of respect for these young people, but the relationship was not without conflict. In a recent interview with Melanie, I asked her how she felt about our relationship. She told me, "*... it was tough at times; I did what you asked of me in Racine and tried to put more of my own spin on organizing in Milwaukee.*" I asked her if she was resentful at times. She said, "*...looking back, I was a young organizer with very little experience, and you provided direction that was needed.*"

An interview with Kate Werning, another Y.E.S. youth organizer, elicited a similar response. She said, "*...I feel really embarrassed about how much I would do differently, about how much I didn't know, and how intense I was, and I could not have worked any harder and tried any harder. It's helpful for me to have a conversation like this, because when I look back on it, I can really see what I would do differently. We, at times, would have disagreements on how to move forward, but it was always about the work.*"

Both Kate and Melanie were extraordinary people who loved the students and had a great deal of responsibility for the rapid growth and political influence of Voces' youth work.

Black, Brown, and White students receiving the
Y.E.S undergrad social justice award
Photo by Al Levie

Social justice organizing had been built into the culture of Horlick. Y.E.S. student activism was paying off. In addition to awards for their activism, students were receiving recommendations that lead to academic scholarships for their work in the community. Their work and relationships helped broaden their networks in ways that offered assistance in pursuing their chosen career paths.

Sisters Gabriela and Berenice Beltran Maldonado representing two generations of Y.E.S. students are standing in front of the Y.E.S. bulletin board which they created

the
STUDENT BILL of RIGHTS
Written by the students of
Youth Empowered in the Struggle (YES)

Student Bill of Rights: A Foundational Document

The Student Bill of Rights was an extraordinarily student-driven, student-created, and student-lobbied document that gave voice to thousands of high school youth in both Racine and Milwaukee. Since its creation, it has served as a framework for identifying the issues that students feel are important and are willing to work for in their educational institutions. Writing the document included gathering the direct input of over 2,000 high school students. It was reviewed and supported by the Racine Education Association and the Milwaukee Teachers Union as well as by individual teachers and community leaders in both Milwaukee and Racine.

Excerpts from the Y.E.S Student Bill of Rights

"Students have a right to organize and have a voice in their school. Students have a right to hands-on and cultural activities to enhance their learning experience, including access to technology, arts, and music. Students' input should be listened to in regard to teaching style and classroom activities in order to craft a classroom environment in which students can learn best."

"Students have the right to learn two languages, including their home language.

Students have a right to freedom from all forms of discrimination. This includes but is not limited to ethnicity, class, sex, disability, pregnancy, religion, native language, sexual orientation, gender expression, housing status, self-expression/personality style or discrimination. "

Student and teacher participants at the student summit where the student Bill of Rights was drafted
Photo by Kate Werning

At the end of her first year of work, Kate Werning came to me and said that she needed guidance on what issues the students wanted to work on. I suggested that we survey the students and find out what *they* believed were important to them. In a meeting with Bob Peterson, the Milwaukee Teachers Union President, he suggested that Y.E.S. crafted a Student Bill of Rights, and that we work collaboratively on it with the students.

Together, Kate and the students developed a questionnaire. They distributed it to all of the high schools that had Y.E.S. chapters. At Horlick, the students' distribution plan included mapping out the school to decide when and where distribution would take place. They attempted to involve students from every grade level and demographic to ensure that the results were representative of the student body. Over 500 survey responses were collected, recorded, tabulated and analyzed.

The drafting of the Bill of Rights took place at a student-led summit with over one hundred Y.E.S. students as well as allies from M.T.E.A, R.E.A, and Milwaukee Public School Board Member, Larry Miller in attendance. Students split into smaller work groups and drafted specific sections of the document with the assistance of Larry Miller and various teachers. It was an extremely fruitful event. Not only did students from diverse backgrounds work together on a common goal, but so did their allies in the community. After the document was drafted there were countless follow-up meetings to revise it and garner additional student and ally input. Once the final document was developed, it was then presented to all of the Y.E.S. chapters for their approval. The students then developed campaigns for both the Racine and Milwaukee school boards to adopt the Bill of Rights as official policy.

The adoption campaigns included recruiting key allies and lobbying school board members. Both the Racine Educational Association and the Milwaukee Teachers Union supported the bill. Individual board members were lobbied prior to the presentation of the bill, and it was put on the official agendas of both school boards.

The first attempt at passage was in front of the Milwaukee Public School Board. The intent to have the resolution serve as an official policy document was in jeopardy. The student Bill of Rights didn't appear to have enough support to ensure its passing, so our main ally on the Milwaukee Public Schools (M.P.S.) School Board, Larry Miller, put forward a resolution to pass the document "in spirit". This was important because it sent a message to the district administration that even without the document's official adoption, the Board supported student voice and organizing.

It passed.

In Racine, however, it was a much heavier lift. Racine Y.E.S. and R.E.A leaders recruited Larry Miller, the M.P.S. School Board Member who had previously championed the bill in Milwaukee to speak on its behalf. During his testimony, was cut off by the R.U.S.D School Board President. The Racine Unified administration and School Board had no intention of even considering the student Bill of Rights. Not only was Larry Miller's democratic right to speak on the matter squashed, but the administration lied, denying ever having had correspondence from Y.E.S regarding the matter. Immediately following this accusation, student youth organizer Kate Werning left the meeting with a couple of students, went directly to the Y.E.S. office and printed off a copy of the email sent to R.U.S.D regarding the student Bill of Rights. They returned to the meeting, armed with their proof. Alexia Gates, a young African American Y.E.S leader walked up to the head table and said *"...they lied, and here is proof."* She proceeded to place copies of the email correspondence in front of each School Board member.

This was done over the resounding pounds of the School Board president's gavel and verbal objections.

Alexia, recalling the day, said, *"... Initially, when Reverend Hargove was pounding his gavel trying to silence me, I felt a wave of different emotions, stemming from angry to empowered. I was angry that after all the hard work we as students put into the letters and efforts of communications with the school board that he would still try to silence us. I felt empowered because it was definitely the right time to be speaking up for our student body and demand their attention and the decency to be heard. We were blatantly ignored with the letters and emails we sent. So, there was no backing down or settling to be silenced anymore. Afterwards, I felt as if a weight was lifted off my shoulders because whether they wanted to hear what we had to say or not... it was finally said and not only did the school board hear it but it was captured by the media as well. I felt relief and happiness because we were standing up for our rights as students and our educational process."*

The R.U.S.D administration clearly demonstrated massive apprehension about passing district policies that were remotely student-centered.

Racine schools were under assault at that time by Robin Voss, a right-wing legislator who represented parts of Racine County.

Don Nielsen, a Racine Unified School Board member at the time, in speaking about the student Bill of Rights and other proposals for which Y.E.S. students had lobbied, recently told me, "*...They [the students] were prepared. They were well spoken. They used their emotions appropriately and effectively and I thought lobbied very well for their position. They weren't listened to all the time but in listening to other Board Members, they were heard.*"

Y.E.S. student leaders were far from crushed as a result of their School Board defeat.

They were motivated.

Their work spoke their truth. The student Bill of Rights shared their vision of a quality education. It was representative of all students. They had worked closely with their allies: other students, teachers, School Board members and people in their community.

They knew who was working with them, and they now knew who was working against them.

Both Racine Unified and Milwaukee School District's lawyers employed the same legalistic arguments and excuses about why their respective school boards could not pass the Student Bill of Rights, claiming that they could be sued.

Y.E.S. members saw the tools that powerful people use to stop change.

In response to the students' Bill of Rights, the Racine Unified School District, in an attempt to show they had a student-centered approach to education, created its *own* process to supposedly garner student input in educational policy. They attempted to organize their own student summit after the school board rejected the Y.E.S. Student Bill of Rights.

The first step was to call a large organizing meeting of students and administrators. Some of the Y.E.S. student leaders were invited to participate. They were furious. They saw it as an attempt to short-circuit student voice and create a process that used the students in an attempt to legitimize District administrative decisions about how they (the students) were to be educated.

Kennia Coronado, a Y.E.S. leader, was one of the students asked to participate in the District's Student Summit. At that gathering, Kennia presented the Y.E.S. Student Bill of Rights to those in attendance. She was shut down by the Assistant Superintendent and escorted out of the hall. I recently asked her to recall what happened, to share with me her thoughts as she presented the student Bill of Rights to the other students with her in that meeting. She said, "*...the district didn't want to really hear our voice. They basically cut my time short. I knew that I would probably face retribution. I knew that they were going to shut me down as I was presenting. I asked the other guest students that were there to basically have my back, and they did. As a high school student, you know you will be punished for advocating for the things you believe in. Students like myself were marginalized in the school. I was thinking, you have all these classes in high school, where you talk about leadership and how you want your students to be leaders in the community. Blah! blah, blah! In the summit they said that they were putting all this into practice. It wasn't going how they wanted it to go even though they designed it. They just put us there to basically go along with what they wanted us to say. And I mean, I think at that point it really pissed me off, right? Because we had been working on our Bill of Rights and we had our own ideas. Their action really demonstrated how afraid people can be of students that are organized and understand power and how to push campaigns forward.*"

I went on to ask Kennia if she would share the repercussions of her actions at the summit. She replied, "*...I got called down to the principal's office and was asked to apologize to the Assistant Superintendent for disrupting the Student Summit.*"

The campaign surrounding the Student Bill of Rights had incredible educational and organizational benefits. Students came together from across racial and economic divides in a safe space where they could explore their interests, and together, they found a vehicle for lifting up their voices. The skills they learned were of the highest educational value. It provided valuable lessons in communication, critical thinking and writing.

Y.E.S. leaders successfully surveyed and communicated with fellow students across multiple schools. They synthesized hundreds of survey results in the crafting of the Bill of Rights. They collaborated with adult educational leaders, clearly explaining their vision for the Bill of Rights while managing to incorporate new suggestions into the document as the process and the document developed. Students prepared and presented the Bill of Rights to the R.E.A. and M.T.E.A union delegate assemblies for support and made public School Board presentations.

Without a doubt, the project impacted the culture of the school. Students from diverse backgrounds found common ground by working together as a group and building their power. Mostly Black, Brown, and White working-class students, who are often viewed by fellow students and staff on the lowest rung of the social hierarchy, gained ground through this work. Their peers and their teachers recognized their leadership qualities. The students in Y.E.S. gained valuable insight into how they were viewed by administration. They came to understand to what lengths they would go to maintain their control and power, to understand that the educational game was not in their favor.

The Student Bill of Rights clearly affected R.U.S.D. Administrative and Board leadership appeared to be threatened by the powerful student voice emerging from Y.E.S. At every turn, the District tried to delegitimize Y.E.S. - to undermine student unity and the collective voice it had developed.

The District's resistance, however, had an opposite effect.

Teachers became actively engaged in helping students develop the Bill of Rights. They assisted the students at their seminar by helping facilitate working groups of students in the crafting sections of the Bill. Students who had engaged in the work helped present the Bill of Rights to the Teachers Union Delegate

Assembly in Racine. Those in attendance at the Assembly were impressed by the presentation of the Bill of Rights. They saw how deeply invested the students of Y.E.S were in their education. The teachers at the R.E.A. Assembly voted to endorse the Student Bill of Rights and stood with them through the process of working towards its adoption at the Board level.

CHAPTER 10

Y.E.S. STUDENTS BUILD POLITICAL POWER

Students, teachers and community volunteers getting ready to canvass the neighborhoods on Election Day. Photo by Keith Kolhman

In Racine, S.U.F.R.I.R and S.U.I.T.S' political non-partisan Get Out The Vote machine had become recognized by all the major political players in the state.

Since 2004, for every election and every school referendum, the students organized powerful Get Out The Vote efforts.

Despite what were already strong efforts in years past, the election of Governor Scott Walker and his assault on Public Education in 2010 changed the civic engagement mindset of the students. They were beginning to experience the direct relationship between the elected officials in their state and the effects of their policies. In 2011, a massive movement developed to recall Governor Walker as well as several other state senators who supported his draconian measures.

Y.E.S. alumni family and friends recall petition dream team
Photo by Al Levie

"I had just graduated from UW-Madison and when my brother, a recently graduated Horlick Y.E.S member, approached me to be involved with the recall of Governor Walker, I jumped at it. It was an energizing experience. The people I met in the neighborhoods we canvassed were incredibly warm and inviting. I was meeting all sorts of people, finding out about other organizations in Racine and just seeing so much energy and potential. The work with Levie and Y.E.S alumni hot-wired and plugged me into the community. The volunteer experience evolved into a full-time paid position with Voces. This further connected me to my community and my family. My parents, who had been

undocumented became local leaders in the struggle for immigrant rights. After Voces, I applied for and was accepted into Law school. I now practice immigrant and labor law in Washington state. Horlick Y.E.S. played a significant part in the adult life choices I have made" Cecilia Anguiano

Y.E.S. alumni collect recall signatures in Pick n' Save parking lot.
They and other alumni collected thousands of signatures
Photo by Tara Harris

For the students, activism at Horlick didn't end upon graduation. Y.E.S. alumni continued to organize their family and friends. They kept answering the call to action in their communities, stepping up to the plate and playing critical roles, such as during the recall efforts in 2011. Together, current Y.E.S. students and alumni gathered thousands of signatures to force a recall election of Governor Walker and Racine County State Senator Van H. Wanggaard. These same former students continued on in their work with Y.E.S. even after the recall efforts, acting as chaperones and volunteers for the subsequent high schooler-led G.O.T.V.

The organization of the students, teachers, parents and community activists who were plugged into the recall election was off the charts. This organization bled into the next Get Out The Vote campaign, which over the years had become a finely-tuned election machine.

Kate Werning, the Voces youth organizer at the time and the Y.E.S. students spent months planning and executing the most effective G.O.T.V. effort in the state. While Governor Walker ultimately retained his job despite the recall efforts, Democrat John Lehman defeated the Racine County incumbent Senator Van H. Wanggaard by just over 800 votes. It was a real nail-biter. Out of all the historic recall efforts around Wisconsin in 2010, only the Racine State Senator was recalled and lost his job.

The student canvassers and the 15,000 doors they knocked on had undoubtedly made a difference.

My interview with former State Senator John Lehman was very revealing. While he couldn't quantify its full impact, he noted his belief that the student effort had a direct impact on his election in 2011. The joint student and alumni effort undoubtedly led to his victory. On election day alone, 350 to 400 students knocked on over 15,000 doors, distributed literature and spoke to residents on the importance of voting. Senator Lehman's tremendous legacy lent name recognition as a Democrat in the city of Racine. His Republican gerrymandered district, however, had nullified his advantage in the city. His victory hinged on massive voter turnout in the City of Racine, an area with traditionally low voter turnout.

The students delivered.

Their contribution increased voter turnout and helped catapult Lehman to victory.

Senator Lehman was the only one of the four Democratic recall candidates across the state to win.

The victory can undoubtedly be attributed to activists, both current students, alumni and community members, who were connected to Y.E.S..

WARD	DAY CAPTAIN	DAY ADULT	A.S. CAPTAIN	A.S. ADULT
1	Lucero Rocha	Marybeth Zuhlke	Chris Reber	Heather Reber
2	Alexia	Ms. Zeien	Chardonnay Wingfield	Julie Fornary & Peter O'Shea
3	Alejandra Sanchez	Mr. Frontier	Angie Perez	Mr. Jensen
4	Janet Serrano	Angelina	Janet Serrano	Angelina
5	Mariana Maldonado	Mark Sommer	Zantasia Johnson	Ms. Blaisdell
6	Victor	Jeff Abel	Shany Carreón	Jeff Abel
7	José Sanchez Flores	Aaron Eick	Isaiah	Rochelle (Isaiah's mom)
8	Berenice Beltran	Contreras	Valeria C=	& Ann Widmer Geisler
9	Tony Ramirez	Julie Harycki	Karina	Kari Steckbauer
15	Viridiana	Jack Bernfeldt	Oscar Peralta	Landry
17	Clarissa	Jay Warner	Bryanna	Sommer
18	Maria Orozco	Mary Minton	Cristian Sotomayor	Ryan Knudson
19	Genesis G.	Steve Platt	Sam K (NHS - leave early)	Mr. Kohlmann
25	Bryanna	Hutton	Luis Garcia	Tom B. & Lund
32	Rebecca	Jen Lerie	Tony	Jason Maxman

G.O.T.V. chart created by Kate and Y.E.S. students
Photo by Josiah Werning

Madison Y.ES, retreat staged action. Organized by Nancy Gibson, drama teacher Photo by Josiah Werning

Education as a Framework for Change

As a result of the impact felt by Y.E.S. students and their action, more refined activities, which required a high level of leadership development and training, began to take shape. The students involved became very skilled at planning and executing major initiatives. The Y.E.S. retreats served to prepare these students for this caliber of work.

Local experts, including teachers and community members, continued to work alongside the students in their efforts. One such teacher was Nancy Gibson, an exceptional theater educator in Racine, who helped students create real-life theater skits for their demonstrations. She assisted in dramatic presentations and exhibitions. Nancy also involved the Y.E.S. kids in her school in her nationally and internationally recognized theater productions that focused on themes of social justice, including the injustices faced by immigrant children and their families.

Community experts in organizing, such as Ed McDonald, a lifelong organizer with a Master's Degree from Harvard University's John F. Kennedy School of Government, led workshops on Saul Alinsky's seven steps of organizing. He assisted students in developing strategic plans and power analyses of their work.

Y.E.S. training also initiated Freedom Schools in which school movement leaders such as Christine Neuman Ortiz, Executive Director of Voces de La Frontera, provided interactive lectures and workshops on the history and current status of the movements in which students were involved.

The educational value of the retreats, freedom schools and collaborative efforts with teachers and local experts was off the charts. History, philosophy, economics and sociology were all incorporated into the curriculum. Young people began to make real connections between their lives and the larger world. They developed an understanding of their collective history. This understanding propelled many of them to seek out careers that further advanced the interests of their communities.

CHAPTER 11

DEFENDING PUBLIC EDUCATION

Y.E.S. activist Lucera Roca testifying on behalf of teachers
Photo by Al Levie

"I mean, I really cared about our teachers, and I felt how this was affecting them, because I saw how they were. This was affecting them in the classroom."

Lucera Rocha

In 2017, The Racine Unified School District, under the staff leadership of Superintendent Lolli Haws and Board President Melvin Hargrove, attempted to take advantage of Governor Walker's anti-education agenda. Statewide, Governor Walker had successfully created a climate that pitted School Boards and administrative leadership against teachers and students.

Walkers' Act 10 gave School Boards the tools to undermine workplace democracy, thereby creating hostile working and learning environments for both teachers and students.

Act 10 prohibited School Boards from bargaining for anything other than wages with their unions, and even that capacity was severely limited. Following the passage of Act 10, employee contracts were replaced with employee handbooks.

In Racine, in the wake of Act 10, following contentious debate and pressure from the community, as well as teachers and students, the Racine Unified School Board incorporated much of the former contract language into its new handbook. The new Superintendent, however, along with a major faction on the School Board, were bound and determined to remove Section 13 from the new handbook. Section 13 outlined a process for requiring input from unions in the District before any changes could be made to the new handbook. It provided for the formation of a handbook committee of both District Administrators and union leadership who would work together in an effort to reach consensus on changes to the handbook.

The vote to remove Section 13 hinged on newly elected School Board member Lisa Parham's vote. Lisa was believed to be strongly influenced and supported by School Board President Hargrove in her election bid. What Reverend Hargrove did not understand was that Ms. Parham was a person of conscience. In fact, Parham's daughter had been a strong, active member of Y.E.S. Parham had proven herself to be willing to listen to all sides on the issues, including to the perspective of teachers and students.

Both leading up to and during the School Board meeting that would decide the fate of Section 13 of the handbook, teachers and students plead their case through phone calls, emails, and testimonies during the public session. Over thirty community leaders, parents, students and education workers testified at the meeting, speaking in opposition to the removal of Section 13 from the handbook. When it came time for the nine School Board members to vote, union leaders had been projecting a four-to-four split, leaving the deciding vote on Ms. Parham's shoulders. When the chair asked for her vote, she paused and asked that they come back to her. Unmistakably, you could hear the disappointment in the Chair's voice as he whispered that she could not in fact do that.

The union projection had been accurate. The vote stood split four to four. The Chair once again called on Parham and asked her to vote. She paused, for what seemed like an eternity, and voted to protect the handbook by voting *"nay"*.

The community in the room, lining the walls and packing every row of chairs, roared in excitement for a people's victory, attributable in no small part to Ms. Parham's willingness to listen to the arguments presented by both students and their teachers.

The moment marked a clear case of students understanding what was at stake for their teachers and standing with them. It left an indelible impression on all that were present.

Teachers and students felt their power.

Proponents of removing Section 13 from the handbook did not forget, either. At the very next School Board meeting, a mysterious envelope was given to the School Board President. It contained evidence that Ms. Parham had faced a felony conviction thirty years prior. As a result of the exposure, she was forced, due to state law, to resign.

It was clearly retribution for her vote.

Following the resounding victory at the School Board level to secure Section 13 in the handbook, the Republican State Legislature passed two bills, specifically applicable in Racine.

The first bill was in response to the vacant seat left by Ms. Parham's resignation. It gave the School Board President the power to unilaterally appoint the vacant seat if the Board had a deadlocked vote in their efforts to appoint a new member. The Racine Unified School Board members cast over twenty ballots without a winner. The anti-teacher, pro-business faction on the Board had their candidate, and the pro-teacher, pro-education faction had theirs.

The vote was deadlocked.

Due to the passage of the new law, the pro-business candidate was ultimately appointed

The second bill aimed at securing an even greater conservative majority on the Board. It completely changed how School Board members were elected and abruptly opened up *all* of the seats for re-election. School Board representation switched from an at-large vote to a geographic one. Previously, all voters in Racine had been able to cast votes for all of the School Board candidates. Now, with the passage of this new bill, voting was relegated to allow only voters from specific districts to vote for their district's specific candidates.

Common wisdom was that the monied interests in Racine County would soon control the School Board with a super-majority.

School Board Re-election
Photo by Al Levie

As a result of yet another massive, student-led campaign to elect progressive candidates following the passage of these two bills in Racine, the conservatives lost eight of the nine seats on the board.

The School Board election was a smashing victory for Y.E.S. and the Racine Teachers Union (R.E.A.) Together, they stood up against powerful business interests in Racine as well as their allies in the State Legislature and won. This election was the largest single display of unity and power thus far exhibited by teachers and Y.E.S. students. They won eight of the nine open School Board seats.

Students, along with R.E.A. leaders, recruited, interviewed and canvassed on behalf of their chosen candidates. Voces de La Frontera Action raised thousands of dollars to finance their election efforts. The students were once again on the front line. In the picture above, all of the students with white shirts were captains of the G.O.T.V. effort. Y.E.S. student captains recruited, trained and canvassed their turf. Over 350 students and 40 adults, mostly teachers, participated in the effort. The captains and volunteers spent weeks canvassing prior to the election. They knocked on doors and spoke to thousands of voters regarding the importance of this election.

Their efforts paid off. Not only were they victorious in winning eight of nine seats, but Pastor Hargrove, President of the board, lost his seat by less than 50 votes.

Block Scheduling: Round 2

Once more, in 2015, the students and staff of Racine Unified found themselves faced with the threat of major change: Block Scheduling.

Without fail, Y.E.S students stepped up and played a central role in bringing teachers, parents and the community together to challenge the district's poorly conceived Block Scheduling proposal.

As previously mentioned, the teacher's union had always been the driving force in unifying educational workers in sharing their perspective on sound educational policy in the district. However, Governor Walker's Act 10 seriously hampered the R.E.A.'S ability to continue doing so. The District Administrative leadership used Act 10 as a means to end collaborative efforts with the union on developing sound educational policy and programs that were in the best interest of the students. Instead, they operated by fiat, bypassing the union and making recommendations to the board with very little union involvement.

The input the District garnered from teachers was often independent of the union. In this new era, teachers were often individually assigned to committees, and they acted on their own accord, not on unity with other teachers in their buildings or with teachers across the district. Their opinions were not grounded in robust discussions with their peers as facilitated through a union-led process.

This new way of business drove a wedge between staff.

At Horlick, many were split over the pros and cons of Block Scheduling. The biggest concern among educational workers, however, was that the proposal was moving way too fast, and that Dr. Haws' hasty implementation was going to have negative results on both students' learning conditions and teachers' working conditions.

Despite the clear lack of planning, Dr. Haws repeatedly insisted that Block Scheduling would begin at the start of the new school year. At a School Board meeting, when questioned by a School Board member as to whether there was adequate preparation for its implementation, Dr. Haws said, "'*...We will make this plane by flying.*" What was not common knowledge at the time was that the district had a much larger initiative in motion, which was the establishment of Career Pathways via an Academy Model at the high school level, and at its core was Block Scheduling.

Both teachers and students were divided on the District's plan. Those in favor argued that Block Scheduling was not a bad idea. Most of those in favor had previously experienced block scheduling while either teaching or learning in other districts. They testified that for some courses, for instance those that are lab or project-based, it made sense, and felt like the right move.

After extensive discussions at Horlick among R.E.A Union and Y.E.S members, a campaign developed. Students and staff asked the School Board to “Wait and Listen”, allowing for time to gather sufficient input from students, teachers, parents and the community.

Y.E.S students, alongside their teachers, decided to develop a Block Scheduling committee to take an in-depth look at the District’s plan and make their own recommendations based on their unique perspectives and needs. After weeks of discussion and planning, the committee had prepared three alternative schedules, each with a detailed rationale, to present to the district in opposition to their “one size fits all” plan.

The Y.E.S task force on Block Scheduling then organized a Town Hall meeting that was attended by over two hundred students, teachers, parents and community members, where committee members gave both an overview of the district’s plan and presented two of their alternatives’ schedules. The audience was given a chance to ask questions before voting on their preferred schedule. One of the committee’s plans was voted through. The meeting was not only well-attended, but highly publicized in the media.

Y.E.S. leader Rubin Ramos moderates town hall meeting at the Racine Labor Council on block scheduling. Seated left to right Jose Rivera, Yobanka Vazquez, Fernanda Jimenez and Tai Klyzub Kalmar. The meeting was sponsored by a Y.E.S. taskforce that included students and teacher.

Horlick Math Teacher and department chair Kristin Althoff presenting Alternative Block Scheduling option #1 at Town Hall meeting
Photo by Al Levie

Horlick Science department chair Steve Zahn raising an important point during the discussion on Block Scheduling
Photo by Al Levie

Following the town hall meeting, Superintendent Eric Gallien met with the Y.E.S. task force, which included students and staff, in the Horlick High School library.

Horlick Y.E.S students and R.E.A. Building President Aaron Eick along with fellow teachers meeting with R.U.S.D. Superintendent Dr. Eric Gallien and his administrative team on their alternative Block Scheduling proposal Photo Al Levie

After passing their Block Scheduling proposal through a vote at their Town Hall meeting, the students and teachers presented their ideas to Dr. Gallien in a question-and-answer session at Horlick. He told us that they would study the proposal and get back to us.

Dr. Gallien did in fact get back to us at the end of the school year. His response was a grand display of power on the part of the District. At a meeting called to discuss the alternative schedule, the dozen or so students and teachers in attendance were met by a room full of Principals and Administrators. The Y.E.S. task force was ultimately told that it was too late in the year to consider their proposal, but that they would consider some of the options put forward by them.

Recently, in an interview with Jose Rivera, a Y.E.S. leader, he said, "*... so we kind of put him on the spot. Right? Yeah, we had an article by the TMJ news outlet. It was also in the Journal Times. That's about as big as you can get here, I mean, that's pretty mainstream - like he had really no choice but to make some kind of statement. The meeting wasn't helpful, I would think, as a person of color, Dr. Gallien would have at least tried to hear out some of the struggles that we were voicing, but it felt like he wasn't. It was just like he was doing his job. It wasn't as if he was committing to making an actual change, or hearing us out.*"

Despite the students', teachers' and parents' efforts, the District rejected their input and ignored their voice.

CHAPTER 12

RESPONDING TO THE RIGHT-WING SURGE

Y.E.S students rally and lobby for Safe School Zone Resolution in Milwaukee Public Schools
Photo by Valeria Ruiz Lira Suarez

"In the hallway you could hear people say things like, 'we will send you to Mexico, where you belong'. Immigrant students and students from mixed-status families were visibly upset. You could feel the tension in the air. Something had to be done."

Geselle Beltron, former Y.E.S. student

Sanctuary Schools

Overnight, with the election of Donald Trump, Geselle's observation was shared by many. Teachers and students could feel the tension in the air during passing time in the hallways of Horlick High School.

Once again, Horlick Y.E.S. rose to the occasion.

They formed a task force of teachers, community leaders and students whose focus was to tackle the threat of increased I.C.E. (Immigration Custom Enforcement) presence in and around the school, as well as to address elevated instances of bullying of immigrant students.

Y.E.S. organizer Elliot Magers immediately contacted the National Immigration Law Center (N.I.L.C) in an effort to find out what was being done nationally to help protect immigrant children from I.C.E raids in the schools. N.I.L.C provided policy language that School Boards could choose to adopt that would keep I.C.E out of the schools entirely.

With this information, the Y.E.S. task force began lobbying the School Board to pass a resolution that would make Racine Unified a sanctuary school district, meaning a district that did not cooperate with I.C.E., where immigrant students were protected from Customs agencies coming in and taking immigrant students for deportation.

The Racine Unified School Board refused to pass it. At the time, the Board Vice-President, Mike Frontier, a longtime civil rights advocate who was sympathetic towards the plight of immigrants and their children, decided not to put the resolution forward. In a recent interview with Mike, I asked him why he did not champion the bill. Mike replied, *"...It was the hardest decision of my political career. Dennis Wiser, the Board President and Lolli Haws, RUSD Superintendent would not support it."* He also went on to say, *"Cory Mason, Current Racine Mayor and at the time Democrat State Assemblyman in Madison also advised me not to support it"* He goes on to recall that Don Nielson, a fellow School Board member told him, *"...I had not been privy to those conversations, but in his meetings with Robin Voss he often implied that if the Board took certain action that there would be budgetary implications."* In effect, the School Board feared that Robin Voss, Republican Chair of the Finance Committee would take vengeance on Racine Unified for acting against his interests. Mike Frontier told me *"... in hindsight I should have ignored the fear of legislative action and introduced the Safe School Zone resolution."*

Mike's experience highlighted for both him, and the students watching him, that bullies will always find something to hold over your head to pressure you into acting in their interests.

Racine Unified School District, after continuing to hear public testimony from parents, students and staff regarding the heightened tension in the building, decided to work with Voces and with Y.E.S. to deal with the potential impact that Trump's election would have on the culture within the schools.

The staff, working with Y.E.S. student leader Fernanda Jimenez, produced a video in which she was highlighted as an undocumented youth. It provided a glimpse into her life as an undocumented student. She recounted what it was like growing up undocumented, and what the election of Donald Trump meant to her and to others in her situation. The video provided education on *Deferred Action for Childhood Arrivals* (D.A.C.A.) and highlighted the fear that the Trump Administration would eliminate the program, which allowed undocumented youth the possibility of gaining legal status.

The video was eventually shown to the over 2,000 district employees during a staff development day. It was also shown during the Voces de La Frontera annual meeting, at which Tony Evers, Superintendent of the Wisconsin Department of Public Instruction and then candidate for Governor was in attendance. Evers asked me for a copy of the video so that he could have it played in other school districts around the state. I informed him that Fernanda did not have D.A.C.A., and that her exposure through the video could potentially lead to deportation. I recommended against it.

A core tenant of my teaching is to protect my students. As an educator, allowing Fernanda to participate in the video put me in direct conflict with my principles. I feared for her status and possible deportation. Ultimately, I decided that it was not my place to make decisions for her and her family. Fernanda's mom had given her permission to participate in the project, and Fernanda decided that she was going to do it.

Recently, I asked her what motivated her to do the video, and she said, "*...Up until that time, I lived in the shadows. I feared exposing the fact that I was undocumented. Right around that time, I read a book that told the story of Malala, an Afghan girl who fearlessly spoke up about the plight of Afghan girls and women. She faced the threat of possible death or disfigurement. I drew inspiration from her strength and commitment. It helped me decide to do the same.*"

Fernanda also stated that, "*...being part of a movement helped me realize that I was not alone, and [that] my teachers, classmates, and community would rally to my defense if there was action taken by I.C.E*"

She knew it would be a public fight. At the Voces annual meeting, her video was shown to over 300 immigrant rights activists from across the state. They recognized her courageous act and would have, at any moment, not only launched a massive, community-wide political campaign to mobilize thousands to come to her defense had she needed it but assembled a legal team to challenge any potential deportation efforts.

It would have made it nearly impossible to deport this courageous young woman.

Fernanda's growing consciousness and willingness to act on behalf of her community was a direct result of the intersection and connection between her family life, her educational experience at Horlick and her involvement in and access to a movement that spoke to her values.

The Y.E.S chapter at Horlick tied it all together and provided an action format for creating change.

Racine Unified Administrative and Board leadership also experienced growth as a result of their involvement in producing the video. It drove home the plight of their immigrant students.

They fully utilized it as both a staff and leadership development tool, showing it at an all-staff in-service and at a public-School Board meeting. Unsurprisingly, the district took a lot of heat for the production of the video. Emboldened in the Trump era, anti-immigrant forces within the community were unrelenting in their criticism of the district for producing the video. To their credit, R.U.S.D. leadership stood strong in their justification of its production and dissemination.

While Y.E.S. students appreciated the video, they would not accept it as a substitute for real policy that addressed their concerns for keeping I.C.E out of the schools. As part of the 2017 May Day march, over 200 strong, the students marched from Horlick to the Racine Unified Administrative offices and demanded a meeting with the Assistant Superintendent, Dr. Eric Gallien. He came to the door and said, *"...we are on your side, there is no need to be confrontational."* The students' response was, *"... then let's meet."* Instead of meeting, the police arrived and the students dispersed. What is interesting to note is that despite the District's supposed sympathy with the plight of the students, the calling of the police put undocumented students in jeopardy. The contradiction was not lost on the Y.E.S. students. While the Racine Unified School Board gave double talk to the students as to why they couldn't pass the Safe School Zone Resolution, the Milwaukee School Board passed an identical resolution put forward by Milwaukee Y.E.S. students. This was a repeat of what had happened some five years prior with the Student Bill of Rights. Milwaukee passed it, and Racine did not. Another generation of Y.E.S. students was being educated on the political nature of the Board of Education.

The mantra, *"[we're] doing what's good for the students"* was tempered by political concerns. In real time, the students were learning about their political reality.

Hunger strikers and supporters
Photo by Al Levie

Deferred Action for Childhood Arrivals (DACA): Under Attack

On Tuesday, September 5th, 2017, Jeff Sessions, Donald Trump's Attorney General, announced the ending of the *Deferred Action for Childhood Arrivals* (D.A.C.A). This program, instituted under President Obama as an Executive Order, essentially provided for immigrants under the age of 31. Those without a criminal record could obtain a temporary 2-year status in order to secure work visas and continue with their education. It was renewable every two years.

With the ending of D.A.C.A., an estimated 1.9 million undocumented youth risked being deported.

Undocumented students at Horlick were shaken to their core.

Fear and uncertainty stuck at the heart of the Latino community. Friends, family members and fellow students could be ripped from their homes and sent back to countries they barely knew. Some had no ties to their countries of origin and didn't even speak the language.

The solution to averting mass deportation lay in the passage of the *Dream Act*, a bill that had been languishing in Congress that would give undocumented youth a pathway to citizenship and pressure President Trump to abandon his plan to end D.A.C.A.

The urgency of the passage of the *Dream Act* could not be understated. However, Congressman Paul Ryan, Speaker of the House, refused to allow a vote on the *Dream Act*. Supporters of the act had lined up 216 of the 218 House member signatures needed in order to force a vote on the matter. They were two votes short. But Representative Ryan lobbied to make sure that it would not come to the floor.

Y.E.S. student leader Fernanda Jimenez, three other D.A.C.A. recipients, Y.E.S. alumni as well as the Y.E.S. organizing director decided to become the local focal point in the campaign to roll back the cutting of D.A.C.A. and secure the passage of the Dream Act. In an incredibly brave act of solidarity, they embarked on a five-day hunger strike to draw attention to the plight of D.A.C.A recipients.

Teachers, church congregations, parents, and community members rallied around the students. They all visited the hunger strikers on a daily basis. They brought them cases of water, games and books and spoke in support at daily press conferences that were held on Monument Square, a highly visible and popular place on Main Street in Racine, Wisconsin. The Olympia Brown Unitarian Universalist Church, located near the protest site, had a history of supporting immigrants, and they welcomed the strikers to sleep in the basement of their church every night.

Y.E.S. hunger strikers leading 700 marchers supporting the Dream Act

On the fifth day of the strike, Y.E.S. and Voces organized a statewide presence in Racine. Over 700 supporters from around the state marched from downtown Racine to the King Statue, about a mile from where the hunger strike took place. They gave speeches, speaking out on the need for immigration reform and called out Representative Paul Ryan for his deeply entrenched and damaging position.

The hunger strikers, along with other activists all over the nation were victorious. On the fifth day of the strike, President Trump announced that he was delaying the elimination of the program by six months. This bought time for a serious court challenge and allowed further work to be done in support of the *Dream Act.*

In addition to averting the D.A.C.A. crisis, the hunger strike educated the public on Speaker Ryan's opposition to the *Dream act.* It turned up the heat. It forced him to make his position public, which he ultimately did. There was significant media coverage. The Racine Journal Times ran front page stories on the strike, highlighting the striker's demands. The strikers produced a full-page commentary in the paper and met with the Editorial Board. Radio and TV also gave it significant air time.

CHAPTER 13
IMMIGRATION REFORM

On an annual basis, Y.E.S. students organized busloads of students to participate in the May 1st immigration reform marches in Milwaukee. Each year, there were upwards of 300 students who attended from Horlick alone.

Locally, Y.E.S. organized activities and events to highlight the plight of immigrants. Attendance at Horlick's annual celebrations, such as Fiesta Patria or Cinco de Mayo ranged between 300 to 500 students and community members. These events provided educational opportunities, providing a platform for students in Y.E.S to share and develop their social justice platform.

These events elevated the community, infusing hope and building power.

The annual Fiesta Patria event was an important Independence Day festivity for most of Mexico, Central and South America. It was a lively, welcoming event, and it connected many Latino parents and families into the school. The Horlick Principal traditionally gave a welcome address, and it served to validate the school as a Latino-centered place in the community.

Fiesta Patria, like so many events sponsored by Y.E.S., simultaneously shed light on issues of importance while providing a safe space for the community to gather and celebrate.

Paul Ryan's Accountability: A Decade of Struggle

For Y.E.S., from 2011 on, the *Dream Act* has been front and center as one of the most important legislative initiatives driving their work. The *Dream Act* provided for a pathway to citizenship and in-state tuition for undocumented youth. It was extremely important to Horlick undocumented students and their families. Passage of the *Dream Act* meant a brighter future for the affected students.

Horlick students in Southeastern Wisconsin lived in Paul Ryan's district. They felt that Ryan was accountable to their community.

Early on, delegations of students met with Congressman Ryan and his staff. They eloquently lobbied him to support the *Dream Act*. He was always very polite to the students, and in fact, supported some aspects of immigration reform. However, despite their efforts, he never voted in favor of the *Dream Act*.

Y.E.S. students' leaders getting ready to go to Paul Ryan's office
Photo by Al Levie

Got Milk Action

The goal of the "Got Milk" campaign was to dramatize and draw attention to the fact that 60% of all milk production in Wisconsin relied on the use of immigrant labor. Immigrants, as essential workers, needed to be recognized and have the same rights as other workers.

Over 100 Horlick students marched in front of Paul Ryan's Racine office prior to delivering the milk cartons to the office
Photo by Al Levie

Student Leaders delivered over 1000 school lunch cartons to Congressman Ryan's Racine office
Photo by Al Levie

When asked in interviews about the most memorable activity they engaged in as Y.E.S. members, those who were students at the time all responded that it was the "Got Milk" campaign. Y.E.S. students collected and washed hundreds of milk cartons from the cafeteria. They then organized their fellow students to join them in their march to Paul Ryan's Racine office, and developed their presentation for his constituent service staff. They also crafted a letter to Paul Ryan and conducted a "Got Milk" postcard campaign. Hundreds of postcards and milk cartons were delivered that day.

As Congressman Ryan gained power in the House, he took a harder position on immigration reform. Despite their efforts, he would not meet with the students or their parents. His rise to becoming Speaker of the House put him in a key role. He had the power to help accelerate and move *Dream Act* legislation forward. However, he refused to allow votes to come to the House.

Y.E.S. student leaders organized and presented at a Town Hall meeting they organized. Over 250 community members were in attendance. National immigrant leaders participated in the event Photo by Al Levie

Y.E.S. and its parent organization, Voces, began to turn up the heat in their efforts to influence public opinion surrounding Paul Ryan's lack of movement on immigration reform. They visited his constituent services office in Racine and participated in larger national delegations of meetings that met with legislators in Washington. When Ryan refused to meet with them and move the legislation forward, Y.E.S. devised forms of more direct action designed to increase public and private pressure on him.

Y.E.S. organizer Elliot Magers leading a Paul Ryan strategy session with Y.E.S. student leaders
Photo by Al Levie

Every action the students engaged in required planning. Professional Voces youth organizers ensured that the students were well-organized and well prepared for the actions and activities they both led and participated in.

Participation in Y.E.S. and in activities such as these strategy sessions provided the students with real, life-long, applicable skills that could be used for both academic and work-related activities.

A prime example is demonstrated in the case of Yasmin Orosco, an alienated youth who dropped out of high school her senior year. In talks with Yasmin, she told me that she came from a hard-working immigrant family who she feels deserved better than working and living in the shadows. She personally saw no future in education. Despite this, Yasmin became an extremely successful adult. She is currently the statewide Assistant Political Director of Voces de La Frontera Action. In that position, she took on the responsibility of overseeing and managing the statewide canvassing operation of Voces. She attributes her success in part to both my classroom, which she considered a safe space, and to her involvement in Y.E.S.

In a recent interview with Yasmin, she told me, *"...Levie, you and Y.E.S. provided me the spark and motivation to do political work for the benefit of my people."* At peak times, Yasmin's supervision includes managing over 200 workers. I asked her if the staff she hired on from Horlick were any different than the other staff. She replied, *"...Definitely, we are hard-bodied. We grew up in the struggle. We understood why [what we were doing] was important. We were fully trained, and [we had] developed the skills in high school that we need today to get the job done, and are doing it for our community. "*

Luis Tapia, Horlick Y.E.S. leader speaking to the Press on the Dream Act
Photo by Al Levie

United We Dream

In 2017, Horlick Y.E.S. students had the opportunity to participate in student-led, United We Dream coalition, which was a national network of high school and college students from across the country fighting for passage of the *Dream Act*. Together, they planned local and national actions in an effort to build public support for its passage. Students in Horlick's Y.E.S. chapter were further involved in a larger delegation of Wisconsin students that participated in the National Day of Action in Washington D.C. Paul Ryan, who represented students and their families in Southeastern Wisconsin, was a central target in their campaign. Through their training and their participation, these students became skilled spokespeople who told their stories well. They traveled, broadening their horizons and became friends with other high school and college students from across the country. That networking, with other students from similar yet diverse backgrounds, had a lasting impact on the Racine students, some of whom had never been out of the state.

CHAPTER 14

RAISING UP BLACK STUDENT VOICE

Y.E.S students in the rally to stand with the family of Donte Shannon
Photo by Al Levie

The merger of Students United in the Struggle (S.U.I.T.S) and Student United for Immigrant Rights (S.U.F.R.I.R) into Youth Empowered in the Struggle meant that the African American students at Horlick had powerful allies in their struggle for justice.

Black students at Horlick were very much affected by abuses of power, both by police across the country as well as in Racine. The killing of Black youth by police hit home when twenty-six-year-old Donte Shannon was shot multiple times in Racine as he ran from police officers. While he was in possession of a gun, it had not been fired. Following his death, Horlick Y.E.S. students organized a large student presence at the marches and rallies that ensued.

The Shannon shooting came in the wake of the national Black Lives Matter movement, sparked by the killing of Trayvon Martin and justified by the Stand Your Ground law passed in Florida, as well as by a whole series of additional police shootings of Black people nationwide. Communities were beginning to formulate an organized response in the wake of these killings to help ensure accountability.

The frustration and alienation of Black youth at Horlick was at an all-time high.

Y.E.S. students, along with the Y.E.S. co-advisor, Aaron Eick, decided that the Black student voice at Horlick needed to be amplified in order to deal with district policy that seemed to be directed towards maintaining order among African American students in the school.

Y.E.S., under the leadership of its African American members, took steps to ensure their voices were heard.

They began work developing a Black Student Bill of Rights, which served as both an agenda for their education as well as an action plan to move the District to consider the demands that were included in the document.

Students planning the Black Student Bill of Rights
Photo by Aaron Eick

At a time when Black students at Horlick felt defeated and isolated, their work on the Black Student Bill of Rights brought them together and infused much-needed hope. It provided them a path to building power and agency through their work.

They were at the center of deciding what they needed and how they were going to get it.

Work sessions, like those used in the preparation of the Black Student Bill of Rights, are a great example of the kind of collaborative, student-driven work developed among leaders and members in Y.E.S.

In preparing the Black Student Bill of Rights, Black students were invited by co-advisor Aaron Eick to brainstorm for the document. Together, they wrote down their ideas on large poster paper. The students were then invited to put sticky notes with a "thumbs up" or a "thumbs down" next to the various ideas they had listed. They were encouraged to leave comments defending their perspectives and opinions.

After two weeks, the sticky notes were taken down, grouped together, listed and labeled to help draw out emerging themes. The themes were then organized, and a Black student agenda was developed.

Our Lives Matter and The Schools We Deserve

Youth Empowered in the Struggle has a history of black and brown unity and trying to make our schools a better place.

In this letter we have incorporated demands from the past with what black students see as immediate problems within the current educational environment.

We demand

A place at the table which includes:

- **A student elected position on the school board**
- **All school and district meetings where policy is being set must have democratically elected student representation that includes students from all groups (not hand picked students).**
- **Students rights posted all over the school that deal with our rights with police, teachers, and administration.**
- **Student Summit where we analyze what is "good" and what is "bad" about our schools and we develop student solutions. These solutions could guide our input at district meetings.**

Immediate problems that need to be addressed.

- **Racial Profiling**
- **Hats and Hoodie Policy (dress code)**
- **End Hall Sweeps**
- **Make school more fun and less like a prison**
- **Healthy and respectful lunch conditions**
- **Less "monitors" and more "advocates"**
- **Staff that feel supported in supporting children rather than teaching to tests**

What we want

- **Integrated interesting classes**
- **More relaxed school environment**
- **More Black staff**
- **School concentration on Justice, equity, and fulfilling potential**
- **Later school start (and less required in-building time)**
- **Caring Teachers**
- **An immediate decrease in arrests, suspensions and in-school suspensions being replaced by a system of support and advocacy**

Student flier, advertising the march to the RUSD Central Office
Photo by Aaron Eick

After the completion of the document and their demands, the next step in the students' campaign was to call a meeting with the Superintendent at the District's Central Office. Y.E.S. organized a march and rally to raise the demand.

Y.E.S. student Chazmire Carothers being interviewed at the march kick-off
Photo by Al Levie

Black Lives Matter march to Central Office
Photo by Al Levie

On the day of the rally, over 200 Black, Brown, and White students marched from Horlick to the Central Office to present their demands.

Rally at Central Office
Photo by Al Levie

"When you called on me to speak, it was very empowering. That small experience has done so much for me in my life. Standing up that day has given me the confidence to deal with and overcome adversity in my life."

STEPHON CHAPMON

Stephon Chapmon was an African American student athlete at Horlick who played both basketball and football. The week before the rally at Central Office, while playing basketball at Franklin High School in a suburb south of Milwaukee, he was at the free throw line when hoards of the opposing team's fans started taunting him, making monkey noises. Their racial abuse continued throughout the game. No moves were made by either the referees or the opposing coaches to put a stop to it.

Stephon's coach, however, gave the team the option to continue playing or to walk off the court; they stayed.

Stephon and his teammates were traumatized. Later, at the rally in support of the Black Student Bill of Rights, I asked Stephon to come forward and say a few words. Courageously, he revisited the incident at Franklin High School and eloquently made the connection between his experience that day and what was happening to Black youth in general.

Recently, in an interview with Stephon, he told me, *"...the event opened my eyes and showed me that I do have a voice - that I do matter. The things that I care about do matter, and I can bring them forward. I became more involved with Y.E.S. and started playing [more of] a leadership role in Y.E.S. activities."*

Racine Journal Times Photo
Y.E.S. leader requesting a meeting over student demands with Stacy Tapp, Racine Unified Communications Director

On the day of the march, despite the fact that the students had filed an official request for a meeting with the Superintendent well in advance, he was nowhere to be found. Stacey Tapp, Communications Director for the Racine Unified School District, was there to tell the students that they needed to leave and that the District would be in communication at a later time regarding a meeting. The students proceeded to hand their demands to Ms. Tapp and marched back to the joint Y.E.S./Voces office where they debriefed, and were served food by the Y.E.S. student leaders.

Aaron Eick, a Y.E.S. teacher advisor, in recalling the debrief said, "*...The students were exhausted and elated. There was a wide variety of students who participated. They included college bound, and advanced placement, as well as those who were habitual truants that would have difficulty graduating; White, Black, and Brown, they all laughed together about how clear we were, how courageous we were, and how fun it was to puff out a collective chest and yet be so sophisticated with our demands. 'Don't suspend us!' 'Treat us like humans!' [they said]. One of my most profound memories of the day centered around one of my African American 10th-grade students. He was extremely bright, often displayed a chip on his shoulder at school, and rarely participated in classroom activity. After the march back from Central Office we gathered at the Racine Labor Center. As he walked in, he said that he was starving. We all could smell food. All the kids entered a room and began to sit down. There were hot dogs, chips, and drinks on the table. The room filled up and people were standing. No one was taking the food. This young man began to push through everyone to get to the table with the food on it. I was about to say '...hey, wait!' I thought in his hunger he and his friends would start eating more than their share before we could evenly distribute the food. I was about to interject with my teacher's voice, asking for a fair distribution of the food. Before I did, he said, 'Hey, who is hungry?' He began serving everyone. He made sure everyone got some. I saw the best in him that day. It was a teachable moment for me. He was invested in the day. He had helped plan and execute the event. He became a leader that day. His dignity and humanity were on full display and I was privileged to witness it. The experience helped me grow as a teacher. He and I grew closer as human beings. The teacher/student divide had been bridged.*"

Following their action at Central Office, Horlick students called for a Black Student Congress to discuss the next steps in their campaign, which included pushing the school to become more responsive to Black student needs. All Horlick students were invited to attend.

Call for a Black student assembly to discuss demands.
Photo by Aaron Eick

A location was set for the Black Student Congress and invites were handed out across the school. The day before the meeting, the school administration changed the venue from a large classroom the students had chosen because it was an environment in which they felt safe to discuss sensitive matters to the cafeteria, a space that both the administration and the police could monitor.

The students refused to change the venue.

Both Aaron and I, the Y.E.S teacher advisors, were told by our administrators that the entire event could not take place unless it was held in the cafeteria. Despite the lack of administrative approval, the students chose to occupy the original classroom for their event. After the students occupied the room, administration used police officers to block access to additional students who wished to participate.

The Y.E.S. organizer at the time, Elliot Magers, assisted the students in a productive meeting. He spent most of his time as a gatekeeper, stopping adults from coming in and disrupting the students' meeting. At one point an administrator came in and declared, *"...this meeting is over."* Elliot turned to the students and said, *"...It's up to you; you to decide what you want to do."* The students chose to ignore the administrator and continued their meeting.

In that moment, the students knew they were doing nothing wrong. Elliot, upon reflection, told me, *"I had never seen such resistance to students meeting and discussing positive changes as I had witnessed for the Black Student Summit."* Administration tried to change the meeting space, they had called the police to stop students from participating, and had forced themselves into the space to announce the meeting was over.

Despite the resistance by the Horlick administration, the students had claimed their space and exhibited their power.

Ultimately, their campaign was a smashing success. The students exercised power in creating their demands, in mass-marching to Central Office and in presenting those demands to the administration through a student congress.

Although the administration never formally met with us, reforms were made in the wake of our organizing.

Following this excellent work, there was a marked difference in how students were treated in the school:

- Hats, pants and student appearance were no longer a reason for a student to be punished.
- There was a decrease in suspensions and arrests.
- Punishment is no longer seen as a positive response in the culture of Horlick staff.

Horlick has not been the same to this day.

Despite the victories, many of the students' major demands were not met.

However, our students felt their collective power.

The students' campaign laid bare the fact that the administration's primary concern was maintaining control. In the wake of the tremendous work infused into Horlick by Y.E.S., the administration remained reactionary. Where there was an opportunity to build upon the emerging student voice, to foster and nurture it, they continued to operate within the status quo, taking credit for work they refused to engage with in a meaningful way.

This unfortunate reality was not lost on the students, but they understood that it was *their* actions that had created the change. In a recent conversation with Tabria Snead, an African American Y.E.S. leader, I asked her how she felt about their efforts and the administration's response. Tabria said, "*... It felt great. I remember the principal taking me to the side and asking me what we expected. Despite the fact that the school did not acknowledge our demands and tried to make it appear as if the changes we were fighting for came from Horlick's administration, it was a definite victory. We were able to get the school to recognize us and not punish us for who we were. We were no longer profiled for what we wore or how we appeared. Our voices were being heard.*"

CHAPTER 15

WHITE STUDENT INVOLVEMENT IN Y.E.S.

As previously mentioned, Horlick High School, like most public and private institutions in the United States, was a racist institution, in that it perpetuated the status quo.

A survey, conducted by S.U.I.T.S. and administered to over 500 students at Horlick, showed that there was a student perception that racial profiling was prevalent in the building.

It was evident for all to see.

As co-chair of the N.A.A.C.P's Education Committee, I often confronted the district on matters of institutional racism. At a meeting between the N.A.A.C.P and the District where Racine Unified was reporting back to the N.A.A.C.P regarding their handling of race relations within the district a Horlick S.U.I.T.S leader accompanied me and presented the students' survey results. The District had no comment at the meeting, but the next day, my principal conducted a formal investigation into the matter. The issues that were raised by my principal had nothing to do with the accusation of institutional racism nor racial profiling in the school. Rather, the line of questioning centered around whether I had participated in the meeting during my duty-free lunch hour and if I had permission from the student's parent to have her accompany me to the meeting.

This story serves to highlight just one instance of the school and the District sweeping the issue of institutional racism under the rug and attempting to silence the messenger.

Although White, working-class students had privilege over their African American and Latino counterparts in the building, it did nothing to elevate their status. The insidious nature of racism is that white privilege pitted poor White students against students of color.

Until the establishment of Y.E.S, there was no organized activist effort to build power among the White working-class students in the building to counteract the effects of Racism among the students at Horlick. There were supportive clubs for marginalized groups of White students, such as the gay/straight alliance, anime and Esports video game clubs, in which many students participated. Still, there were no efforts to help these students collectively deal with their issues as was done with the students of color.

White student involvement in Y.E.S. began gradually, with social justice teachings and classroom discussions which a handful of teachers injected into their curriculum. These lessons and conversations allowed students of color and the White population at Horlick to engage with one another.

Additionally, staff members who remained involved in the struggle alongside their students by participating in events and meetings helped recruit White students to join them in activities sponsored by S.U.I.T.S. and S.U.F.R.I.R.

At first, the White students were not on the ground-floor of the organizing efforts for activities such as the immigrant rights marches or the Black Lives Matter protests, but they participated as allies.

Sisters in the Struggle: Raina Murillo, Anna Huth
and Sara Sandgren getting ready to canvas
Photo by Al Levie

However, the Get Out The Vote campaigns for elections and school funding referendums changed that.

White students went from just being allies to brothers and sisters in the struggle. They were not, however, always welcomed with open arms. Anthony Brulport is an example of this reality. He grew up in Arizona and had started attending Horlick in 10th grade. He struggled to establish relationships with other students. In a recent discussion with him, he told me, *"...I could understand they [students of color] did not accept me right away because people of my color were putting them down. They assumed we were just part of the problem. I grew up in a poor mixed neighborhood in Arizona. My best friend at 8 [years old] was Mexican and I saw how my friend was treated differently. As I grew older, I began to understand that I had White privilege. At Horlick, the African American and Latino students were treated differently. It didn't sit well [with me]. I just kept volunteering to help out and speak out, and eventually, I was accepted as a brother not as a White person".*

Anthony was an extraordinary young man, and he proved it time and time again. In one of my classes, during a discussion on discrimination in housing and the civil rights fair housing tests, Anthony remarked that the same thing was happening at Horlick. During that particular class, by coincidence, I sent an African American student to the library to get a book. He quickly returned to the room and said that the librarian stopped him from going in because he didn't have a pass. Anthony told the class that that was, *"bullshit."* He could get in. So, I sent Anthony to the library without a pass to pick up a book.

He came back with it.

The African American students saw his outrage at the blatant inequity in treatment between himself and his Black classmate. It was then that trust was built. Anthony became an accepted leader in their struggle. With the establishment of Y.E.S. in 2011, Kate and I sought out ways to increase White student involvement and to build their leadership. In selecting students to participate in our annual trips to Washington D.C, we intentionally included White students who had demonstrated a commitment to work on social justice issues side by side with the students of color. The Y.E.S.

Student Bill of Rights, a foundational document, broadened the appeal for White student involvement. Students gave massive input across racial, gender and economic lines.

Over the years, efforts surrounding Block Scheduling, the handbook, and the Student Bill of Rights all involved the participation of many White students.

White students working with students of color on social justice issues was life changing.

Many of the White students grew up in the same neighborhoods and were friends with the students of color. However, being part of a social justice movement with their peers gave them a much deeper understanding of the injustices of the systems that surrounded them.

It sparked a desire to change them.

Dylan Straube, a Y.E.S. leader who graduated in 2019, shared with me in a recent interview how his education and experiences in social justice movements changed him. He said, *"...I grew up in a diverse neighborhood, but never really understood Racism. In Mr. Eick's African American History class, I learned about systemic racism and how it played out internationally, nationally and in Racine. It motivated me to be involved in the Black Student Bill of Rights campaign and then I became heavily involved in Y.E.S. I developed an admiration for the students of color. They had all the things to deal with that I had [had to deal with], such as homework. But they had another layer of things to deal with such as racial profiling and renewing DACA on a yearly basis, or whether their status would keep them from attending college. The insights I gained in school and [in] my involvement in Y.E.S. has awakened a sense of social justice. I just graduated from Parkside and will be pursuing a career in law. I would like to either specialize in civil rights law or immigrant law."*

Talitha Gudal, the salutatorian of her graduating class and a strong White Y.E.S. leader said, *"Before my involvement with Y.E.S., I really struggled with empathy. I really didn't think much about people. It sounds really bad, but I just was kind of always in my own world. I was an introverted person. I didn't think about my impact on the world or my community. Working with Y.E.S. really helped me connect with other people and make friends and do something bigger with my life than just being this student that goes to school, and then goes home and does hours of homework and doesn't talk to anybody. It got me out of my shell and I became more extroverted."* She went on to say, "*...My participation in the election efforts were life changing. I came from a working-class background and sometimes we were poor but we always had a door on our house. We always had windows. We lived in a part of town which was relatively safe. In my canvassing with my fellow students, I was exposed to genuine hardships. In my conversations with people at the doors, however, I saw a huge level of community and people helping each other and working together to make things better. I didn't see this in my mostly White neighborhood."*

Talitha went on to tell me, "*...as an adult I realized that fighting racism was my responsibility in my community. I recently attended a Black Lives Matter rally in my community. I listened to white speaker after White speaker not quite hitting on the points that I had heard from rallies that included Black speakers. After the rally I respectfully approached the leaders and offered up some strong suggestions which included networking with and inviting Black folks involved in the movement to participate in their efforts. They seemed very receptive and thanked me."*

Without a doubt, the experience Talitha gained in Y.E.S. gave her the tools to step up as a leader in her adult life. Talitha is studying to be a teacher, and her involvement with Y.E.S. helped put her on that path.

In this section, I have highlighted three of the six White students that I interviewed for the book. Some are quoted in other sections. There were similar patterns to their testimonies. All of them shared with me that their outlooks and their friendships were broadened as a result of their involvement with students of color in fighting for justice and that they gained a sense of confidence by participating in events in the community. For most of them, like many of their brothers and sisters before them, participation in Y.E.S. kindled a passion for social justice that influenced their future career paths.

CHAPTER 16

SOLIDARITY: A TWO-WAY STREET

Al Hutton, a Horlick High Guidance Counsellor, takes a personal day off work and marches in solidarity with his students
Photo by Al Levie

"My initial involvement with the students, chaperoning their Get Out The Vote, attending the Fiesta Patria at the school, marching with them on May 1st for immigrant reform, led to students trusting me enough to engage in conversations about the reality their parents faced. Hearing about the graveyards in the desert and other stories of the hardships gave me the resolve to do more. When you asked me to participate in a civil disobedience action in Paul Ryan's Office, I didn't hesitate."

Al Hutton Horlick High Guidance Counselor
with 41 years of tenure in RUSD

Al Hutton, an extremely popular teacher and counselor at Horlick had always gravitated towards student organizing.

Over two hundred students and community members held a rally in support of Al and three other community members who were arrested for conducting a sit-in protest to draw attention to Paul Ryan's conscious act to block forward motion on the *Dream Act.*

Al Hutton's decision to get arrested on behalf of immigrant students had an undeniable impact on the culture of Horlick. The display of staff solidarity following his arrest was astounding. On the day after the arrests, during my lunch period, I solicited my colleagues to contribute towards the $273.00 ticket Al had received. In total, we contributed $271.00 towards his ticket.

The fact that so many of his colleagues gave ten to twenty dollars was a real tribute to Al and to his character, but also a strong indicator that the culture of Horlick had shifted to one of solidarity with its immigrant students.

Al was not the only teacher at Horlick who, through their actions, showed strong support for the students' social justice efforts. Many attended the students' school events, served on joint Y.E.S./ teacher task forces, participated in the Get Out The Vote efforts and made linkages between their work in the community and the students' work.

Diane Lange, a former Horlick Consumer Education teacher, quietly participated in many Y.E.S. school-based and community activities. Her Consumer Education kitchen was often used for Fiesta Patria, to cook or warm food. She participated in major marches each year for immigrant rights, and always helped out with the Get Out the Vote student efforts as an adult chaperone. However, her most significant acts of solidarity with the students and their immigrant families were done through her church. As the chair of her congregation's social justice committee, she got involved in supporting the students, their families, and their community. When the students and other D.A.C.A. recipients held a five-day hunger strike on the *Dream Act*, her church, under Diane's advice, extended its hospitality and made the students comfortable by providing a place to sleep overnight. Diane also led a massive fundraising effort in her church to pay for seats for students to ride buses to Washington D.C for various *Dream Act* activities. She and another member of her church even chaperoned one of the trips. Over the years, Diane has also accompanied undocumented immigrants to court for deportation cases. Furthermore, she created a network of people to become involved with her, further extending her outreach in Racine.

Immigrant students at Horlick and their families knew they had an ally in Diane. By association with her work, Horlick became a more welcoming place for the Latino community.

From the beginning of his tenure at Horlick, Aaron Eick, a fellow Social Studies teacher, worked to connect with the students. As a new teacher, during his prep hour, Aaron would sit in my class on a daily basis to observe how I built relationships with my students. It became apparent to him that the connection that I had with them went beyond classroom learning.

The professional distance he was taught to maintain in his teacher training did not exist in my class. Authentic conversations were happening - conversations that transformed into real action. Aaron's curiosity led him to begin participating in the club activities that I advised. At first, he simply attended the events in a show of support. However, it quickly evolved. He soon began assisting the students in their planning and organizing.

Aaron is now the co-advisor to the Y.E.S. club.

Aaron, raised in a solid union household, understood the meaning and value of worker solidarity. His mother was an active teachers' union member and his father a union policeman. At Horlick, he was a strong union member and served many terms as union President. He worked tirelessly to build power among the teachers so they could work with dignity on the job, affecting reform that would enhance the quality of education the students received. His involvement with Y.E.S. and its activities brought him to the realization that student voice is critical for meaningful educational reform to take place. Through his teaching and his work with staff, Aaron strengthened and promoted the connection between the teacher's union and Y.E.S., acting as a bridge between both groups. He brought the teachers' issues to the students and the students' issues to the teachers. Over time, they began to understand their commonalities and the struggles they shared.

Through his work with both the students and the staff, Aaron breathed life into the saying, *"... [the] teachers' working conditions were students' learning conditions."* Teacher campaigns became student campaigns, and via versa. The connection between the teachers' union and Y.E.S. had a far-reaching impact on the culture of Horlick. A mutual respect developed, and teacher/student solidarity blossomed.

The three teachers highlighted in this section, while showing extraordinary solidarity with the students, were by no means the only teachers to have done so. There were countless Y.E.S.-initiated activities that teachers not only showed up for, but actively participated in. They often took on speaking and leadership roles and took unpaid personal days in order to participate. In addition, many teachers regularly involved their families, further building the network of support in our school and in our communities.

These acts of solidarity by Horlick staff created undeniable synergy with their students.

The relationships they developed had a spill-over effect. Building relationships so deeply rooted in mutual respect became real and meaningful to the teachers and the students. As a result of the tremendous work done together by both staff and students on social justice issues, parents who had often felt apprehensive or fearful now saw school as a safe place for their children and for their families. They knew there were staff in the building that would look out for and protect their children.

CONCLUSION

Retirement morning send-off for Al Levie
Photo by John Fleishner

In 2019, after 19 years of teaching, three months before retirement, my fellow teacher and Y.E.S. advisor Aaron Eick organized a Friday Morning send-off. Y.E.S. students, along with staff and community members attended.

It was a touching event.

Memories flooded back to me of all the activities and actions in which I had participated with the students over the years. I reminisced about the particularly defining moments, times when students, by virtue of their actions, became more than who they had been. I also thought about how student voice and agency had crept into the teachers' consciousness- how the teachers' perceptions of their students had changed by engaging with their personal stories - how all of their shared experiences shaped and affected their newfound relationships with them.

I was honored by their recognition of my work that day.

Those accolades, however, were not the only that I had received for the work I had done over the years. Among the honors presented to me was *The Hispanic Unsung Hero Award* from the King Center, an award from the N.A.A.C.P. for the work I did with African American Youth. Additionally, I received two *Advisor of the Year Awards* from Voces de La Frontera, *Everyday Hero* recognition from the Shepherd Express, and a *Humanitarian of the Year* award from Gateway Technical College.

In truth, I was only receiving the awards for the work done by the students, their parents, teachers and the community. As an educator with a social justice consciousness, I simply integrated a social justice component into my classroom curriculum. In doing so, I helped shift the culture of the school and networked in ways to connect my students with their communities. In effect, I provided the pathways for the students to act on their own behalf. As every good high school coach or teacher did, I was intentional about getting to know my students.

Every school day was a learning experience for me. I learned about who my students were, as individuals, about their dreams and their aspirations, and the many obstacles to their success.

What became apparent to me early on in my tenure at Horlick was that the school system was stacked against working class and poor students; it was an impediment to reaching their goals. The classes were segregated by perceived ability level and interest; there was heavy tracking in place, and expectations of what students could achieve were grounded in those tracks to which they were relegated.

While there were many top-down attempts by the administration district-wide to raise up the lower-achieving individuals and groups of students, by and large, they failed. The Racine Unified School District remained a district rooted in institutional racism and classism; there was a constant perpetuation and reproduction of the status quo with regard to student achievement and academic success.

On an ongoing basis, I was amazed at the rigidity of the system. While every new administration espoused student-centered learning with educator input, there were limited attempts to seek out that input by administrators. As evidenced in the book, the District consistently rejected or dampened down authentic student voice, and they used the students to legitimize their own perspective and practices.

A glaring example of this happened in the review process of the student handbook. At the direction of the school board, Y.E.S. was asked to participate in revising the old handbook. While the students in Y.E.S. offered their perspectives at the meetings, they were ultimately never presented with the final handbook draft for their consideration. Most of their suggestions were ignored without explanation, and to add insult to injury, Y.E.S. was listed in the handbook as one of the cooperating groups who had served to create it.

For this book, I interviewed Trish Young, one of the two Y.E.S. student participants on this handbook committee. She had this to say about her participation on the committee: *"...It felt like what we were putting down in that handbook was very important and powerful. However, no matter how coherent or intelligible our conversation was, no matter how much they agreed with us, face to face in the room when it came down to it, what we had to say didn't matter."* She went on to add, *"...District leadership did not include us in putting together the final draft of the handbook, [and we] had not seen it before approval; most of the students' suggestions were not included."*

For the most part, positive change that impacted teaching and learning at Horlick came about as a product of active organizing. Organized students and teachers involved their peers, the parents, and community members. Together, they swam against the current. Their ideas, however, were not accepted without struggle. They developed a culture of resistance and resilience. They held their heads high and came to an understanding that it was the system that was failing the students and the staff, not the other way around.

Across the board, those who were involved in the struggle to improve conditions had a meaningful high school experience. In interviews, student after student expressed the same thoughts as Breana Stevens, a former student activist and now a teacher in Seattle, Washington. In a recent interview with Breana, she spoke with frustration about the culture of the school at Horlick before the students began to organize. She highlighted the fact that opportunities for self-expression and awareness were limited, that students had no place to share their experiences or change things in the school and in the community. She told me, "*...Student organizing gave you a chance to know the people you were around, but also you could do things that were impactful and meaningful for those who otherwise would not have gotten much attention.*"

Breana pointed out that the students were a valuable, untapped resource in the school for making positive change. In a school, there are thousands of people, all from different backgrounds, who care about their education and each other. In our conversation, when referring to the work of S.U.F.R.I.R. and S.U.I.T.S, she went on to say, "...it *showed students what organizing looked like because oftentimes, we thought if you wanted to get things done you need some sort of leader, you need some sort of group of teachers or adults to tell us what to do. Our work was in the students' hands and students were the driving force.*"

Breana, like her brothers and sisters in the struggle, came to understand that by students organizing, there existed many opportunities to create and continue re-creating the spaces they occupied.

Kamayla Richardson, a student leader at Horlick who went on

to become a very successful owner of a day care center providing services for over eighty children, was a strong example of the resistance and resilience built up in these student activists. Up until her involvement with S.U.I.T.S and S.U.F.R.I.R, she described herself as, "*...a negative leader in the school.*" She said, "*...Kids would follow me. As hard as I tried, I could not find a place at the school that spoke to my needs, and I would act out in negative ways, resisting what I believed to be an institution that did not speak to me or care about me or others like me. When I got involved with S.U.I.T.S. and Y.E.S, all of this changed. I was involved with the wrong crew, and I noticed people were following behind me, and not for good things. Other students knew that I had this power to get people to do things.*" Other students, like Xavier Marquez, leader of S.U.F.R.I.R, recognized her leadership status among the African American Students and recruited Kamala to become involved. Kamala's impact in the school shifted in new and powerful ways, and her influence helped draw many other students to meaningful Y.E.S. activities. Her participation as a student activist changed her, and it changed how people viewed her. She went on to say, "*...Before my involvement, I was seen as disrespectful, doing negative things, but once I started to be involved, I started gaining respect from other individuals. A lot of teachers [came] to me and said, 'Kamala, you should do this.'*" Staff no longer saw her as a hot-head with a chip on her shoulder. They began to see her in a different light- as a student with a lot of potential.

In Part 1 of the book, I talk about my beginning years as a teacher at Horlick. I recount the connections I made with my students, both in the classroom and in the community. I shared the experience of watching student power and teacher buy-in emerge both in my classroom and in our school. I explored the development of Latino and African American-based organizing and the establishment of S.U.F.R.I.R and S.U.I.T.S as well as the eventual convergence of the two. Y.E.S. was the product of that convergence.

In Part 2, I focus on how Y.E.S. broadened its issues to school-based organizing, dealing with issues ranging from curriculum to District governance. We also looked at the deepening well of alliances the students built with both their teachers and the community at large.

In preparation for this book, I conducted over fifty interviews with former students involved in organizing efforts. Additionally, I spoke to eighteen teachers, administrators, school board members and community leaders. The students I interviewed had been at Horlick between 2003-2019, spanning the entirety of the 16-year period I spent involved with student organizing. It would have been impossible to capture all of the thinking and experiences of the students in one book, for our conversations were lengthy, deep and rich. I have, however, tried to provide a flavor of their analyses of their experiences and their recounting of the activities they were involved in as well as their observations and interactions with teachers, school board members and people in their communities.

My conversations with all of these remarkable people have helped me capture the effects of student and teacher organizing the school system and the community at large.

As a result of my work both as a teacher and in writing this book, here are some truths I have uncovered:

1. Relevant classroom activities as well as the trust and relationships I built with the students sparked their desire to become involved with issues that were important to them.
2. Student activist clubs provided students with a space in which they felt safe and valued.
3. The community activities in which students were involved changed them. It made them feel like their voices were heard. They became more self-assured and confident.
4. The skills acquired through organizational work and activism helped students become more successful at school and in their careers.
5. Active involvement with their peers, teachers, family members, community organizations and political leaders gave students a larger view of the world and helped them shape

their values. It developed career and life paths that might not otherwise have been apparent.

Throughout the book, quotes from students, teachers, school board members and people in the community capture a small slice of the impact that student activism had on Horlick students, the school, the District and the community.

Student organizing did not stop with my retirement.

Currently there are over fourteen Y.E.S. chapters in high schools and four chapters in colleges between Milwaukee and Racine. The work continues to have a positive impact on the cultures of the schools and communities where they have been established.

ADDENDUM

Mural painted by Art teacher and Artist John Fleissner and assisted by Y.E.S. students
Photo by John Fleissner

Today, under the local teacher leadership of educators Aaron Eick and Jessika Malacara, as well as the additional assistance of staff leadership and Voces Youth Organizing Director, Ari Antreassan, Y.E.S. continues to be a dynamic force for change.

The students and teachers at Horlick continue to jointly organize on issues that matter.

The student organization of Y.E.S. and the teacher's union in the building continue to work together and develop strong teacher/ student relationships.

For instance, the Covid pandemic in 2020 impacted how teaching and learning took place in the District, but it did not impact students and teachers working together.

Horlick Y.E.S. leaders making a statement of solidarity for Black Lives Matter
Photo by Aaron Eick

Since my retirement, there are many examples of continued work, such as:

Covid 19 work

In 2020, Y.E.S. developed and proposed The Smart Start Plan for returning back to school in the wake of a global pandemic. It included input from both teachers and students.

The plan included placing a moratorium on all programs not directly related to the education and well-being of students. It highlighted the importance of taking students' and families' needs into consideration with regard to the delivery of instruction during an unprecedented time in public education. It provided the necessary leverage to teachers to help ensure that they would be given the choice to teach from their assigned school building or from home, and finally, it proposed a full community, "all hands-on deck" approach to being there for our students and families.

Jointly, teachers and students in Y.E.S. presented it in an op-ed piece in the Racine Journal Times. The District ultimately adopted some of their recommendations, but not all.

Essential Worker Protection

During the pandemic, workers in the essential industries, such as those in the meat packing plants, were contracting and dying from the spread of Covid-19. Workers believed proper safety procedures were not in place to protect them. Y.E.S. organized students to support essential workers in their struggle to make their places of employment as safe as possible. They participated in marches and rallies in support of workers in an effort to put pressure on major local employers to institute adequate safety protocol procedures that would contain and prevent the spread of Covid-19.

Racine Mayor Cory Mason doing a sendoff to students preparing to canvas on election day
Photo by Ari Antreassian

Election Work

Y.E.S did not let the Covid-19 pandemic stop them from organizing and working together to turn out the vote in their communities for a critical election in April of 2020. Students organized Zoom calls and spent their days at home talking to voters, asking them to vote *"yes"* on a referendum that would provide $1 billion dollars over the next thirty years to the Racine Unified School District. This referendum was won by only four votes after a recount and had been challenged and upheld by the courts.

In this same Spring election, Y.E.S. helped to elect Edwin Santiago, the first Puerto Rican Alderman in the history of the City of Racine.

Youth Protection Resolution

In 2021, as a direct result of student activism and lobbying in Y.E.S, the City of Racine adopted a resolution that established as city policy an alternative to ticketing and financial penalty procedures for in-school truancies. Instead, the city approved community service as an alternative to tickets, whereby students were asked to serve ten hours of service in their communities. Recently, in a conversation with Rob Weber, Racine Municipal Judge, he told me that this resolution has helped him sleep at night. Oftentimes these fines, issued to lower income students, went unpaid and as a result, juvenile offenders would not be able to obtain drivers licenses. Even more seriously, the truancy tickets would turn into warrants for students upon turning eighteen years old.

The resolution for community service was developed and lobbied for by the Voces/Y.E.S. demilitarization committee. Horlick Y.E.S. leaders played a strong role in securing this victory.

Horlick Y.E.S. leaders involved in the campaign to open the bathrooms
Photo by Aaron Eick

In-school issues

Y.E.S. continues to be a voice for the students and a force for change with Horlick.

A recent, successful in-school campaign exemplifies their work. Aaron Eick, the current teacher co-advisor for Y.E.S told me, "... *In the beginning of the 2002-2023 school year, Y.E.S students conducted a survey of over 1,000 students, asking them [about] the most pressing issues. The students overwhelmingly said [the] locked bathrooms. Horlick Y.E.S. launched a campaign to open the bathrooms."* Aaron, in his proud recounting of the campaign said, "*...They first requested a meeting with the unionized Horlick education workers and discussed a joint solution to prevent locked bathrooms. They developed a joint proposal with the teachers. They then went to the Horlick administrative team with a proposal. After several meetings, it was clear that they (the administration) were not willing to entertain our ideas or change their bathroom policy. We pressured our admin by going over their heads to District leadership. They finally bent to our demands. Students were elated, and the rest of the year was a better, more relaxed year because Y.E.S. [had] organized."*

In my recent conversations with the advisors, staff and student leaders at Horlick, it has become clear that student organizing has evolved. It has become part of the DNA of the school. Many of the new freshmen already know about the activist organizing efforts and have signed up to be part of it.

When Y.E.S. initiates an activity or sparks a response to a situation, students join in and they are hopeful that their voices will be heard. The administration at Horlick takes Y.E.S' suggestions seriously; they know the students will not allow issues to go unresolved.

Additionally, the link between Y.E.S. and Voces de la Frontera has deepened over time. Horlick students are now an integral part of the Voces Action electoral strategy. Their Get Out The Vote campaigns and other election efforts are not done in isolation, but rather in total lock step and coordination with Voces.

STUDENT VOICES

Student activism, under the guidance of educators skilled in grassroots organizing like Mr. Levie, changed the trajectory of my life. My involvement in youth organizing socialized me into understanding that I had agency over the conditions of my life and the lives of others in my community. It shaped my research agenda as a PhD and taught me the importance of educators in the mentorship of emerging generations.

Kennia Coronado, PhD, Philosophy (Class of 2012)

Mr. Levie was a teacher that believed in all of us. He inspired us to follow our dreams no matter how big or small. Mr. Levie showed us a world outside of Racine, Wisconsin. We always knew we could count on him to guide us to success.

Brittney Callaway, Special educational teaching assistant (Class of 2009)

Mr. Levie was a teacher that cared about all of us. Race, Color, nor Ethnicity mattered in his classroom, everyone was loved. He gave us experiences that helped us build power and become successful adults. He played a vital role in preparing me for college, I received many scholarships due to my leadership experiences and actions while working with Voces.

We will never forget that our voices MATTER and when you keep a "yes I can" attitude, anything is possible! Si se, puede!

Alexia Gates, Business Owner (Class of 2013)

Mr. Levie mentored, inspired and empowered a generation of students to become confident and passionate leaders of today.

The skills he helped us develop in grassroots organizing will stay with us for life

Xavier Marquez, Builder (Class of 2006)

Mr. Levie was an amazing mentor and teacher to so many students. He genuinely cared about all his students and seeing them succeed. His wealth of knowledge and experiences helped us become successful adults.

Berenice Beltran Maldonado, Masters of International Affairs at Penn State University (Class of 2014)

Being a part of Mr. Levies' class positively impacted my classmates and myself. We had the opportunity to learn about social, educational & economic systems overall. We learned how to use our education to advocate for what we believe in and express our thoughts, our truth, our struggles, the barriers instilled in the system and overall, we were able to express ourselves.

Breana Horton, Clinical Therapist, MSW (Class of 2014)

Mr. Levie always encouraged us to move forward, face our challenges and never feel alone.

He gave us experiences that helped us build power and become successful adults

Viviana Pastrana (Class of 2006)

Being in Mr. Levies' class and a part of student activism taught me that even as students, our voices matter and can make change happen.

Cecilia Leal, Educational Assistant and Mother (Class of 2007)

Levie was one of the ones who paved the way for me so I could help in the fight for the rights of others.

Gabriel Coronado, Esq. Attorney (Class of 2011)

Mr. Levie made students discover their own potential by letting them know they are indeed seen.

Geselle Becerra, Customer Experience Banker (Class of 2018)

Being a first-generation student in Mr. Levies' class allowed me to not only share about my culture but learn about others cultures as well. It made me appreciate my culture even more.

Ruby Ruvalcaba, Performance & Quality Assurance Coordinator (Class of 2010)

This white man stood up for me like I was his own child. Now I'm a master's holding RUSD teacher, when I could have been expelled during my last year in high school.

Maranda Mack, Racine Unified School District Teacher (Class of 2006)

Mr. Levie believed in making sure his students acquired knowledge, competence and virtue via experience. He gave me a glimpse of what I didn't know would be part of my future and a hope and drive to excel in his class.

Jarasha Williams, Minister of God/Certified Nursing Assistant/ Entrepreneur (Class of 2010)

Student organizing at my high school brought me closer not necessarily to the problems, but to the people. I was aware of various injustices, but building invaluable connections between people gave me the courage and confidence to actually take a stand.

Breana Stephans, 5th grade communications and literacy teacher (Class of 2009)

Working with Mr. Levie has turned us into an army of dreamers, an orchard of seeds ready to sprout and bloom for another world, another way of doing things that we now know is possible.

Gabriel Hernandez (Class of 2015)

www.ingramcontent.com/pod-product-compliance
Ingram Content Group UK Ltd.
Pitfield, Milton Keynes, MK11 3LW, UK
UKHW062259290726
14090UKWH00017B/780